The Peril of Atomic War

A geostrategic reflection on the conflicts of the 20th and 21st centuries

Pablo Rafael Gonzalez

Legal Deposit: If25220033001923
ISBN 980-12-0347-1

This edition was made by CreateSpace in May 2015 in the United
States of America.

How the scarcity of natural resources, especially water, food, and oil generates scenarios of conflict that might lead to limited wars in some regions or to a global conflict is the main theme of this book.

The author makes a historical re-count showing how economic crisis, inflation, unemployment and the struggle for natural resources were determining events in the great conflicts of the 20th century and stated that if it occurred in the past it could be repeated again in the 21st century.

The book claims that the crisis of natural resources due to overexploitation and pollution will be more intense in the coming years.

It shows how the conflict with North Korea had its origin in the absence of oil and food and demonstrates how the confrontation with Iran is also caused by the energetic problem.

The book asserts that water is the most scarce and valuable resource in the 21st century and how this fact will cause serious problems for world food production.

The author reveals the fact that humanity has barely 30 minutes to avoid an atomic war if by any error any of the nuclear countries believe that is being attacked.

The book presents a message of hope and affirms that the only way to preserve life on the planet is to stop the construction of nuclear and bacteriological weapons, to halt the destruction of forests and to begin a global campaign for reforestation, to have a drastic decrease of the emission of greenhouse gases into the atmosphere and to start the preservation of water, avoiding contamination.

How beautiful upon the mountains are the feet of him that bringeth good tidings, and that preacheth peace: of him that showeth forth good, that preacheth salvation, that saith to Sion: Thy God shall reign!

Holy Scriptures
Prophecy of Isaiah, Chapter 52.7

Humanity wishes happiness; the essential condition for obtaining happiness is peace, because without peace happiness is not possible. Peace is, then, the key for human progress and happiness.

In order to reach peace it is necessary that everybody is aware of the conflicts that might cause war. This work intends to help to a better comprehension of the situations that can threaten peace, hoping to create a better world with more justice.

Has the world overcome the peril of nuclear war? What is the real situation of the natural resources? Can the crisis of natural resources lead to local conflicts or a global confrontation? Is Russia behind Iran? Is China the big shark that is behind the sardine that is North Korea? These are some of the responses that this essay attempts to answer.

To de Lord of Universe

To my beautiful and beloved children

Introduction

Nobody can predict the future with accuracy. But the prospective and the rational methods of analysis ---the possibility of scientist prediction--- help to build scenarios that sometimes are very close to reality.

In the first decades of the 21st century the world is facing an unprecedented situation: the threat of nuclear weapons by emergent powers.

The menace of North Korea and Iran is true; it is something verifiable and not only speculations. These countries have developed an important nuclear power and the means of using them at long range.

On Saturday, April 4, 2009, North Korea fulfilled its purpose of launching a rocket of long reach into space. The remains of the rocket fell on the Sea of Japan and the Pacific Ocean.

Official reports from Pyongyang said that the rocket transmitted the favorite tunes of the country's founder Kim IL Sung, of the current leader Kim IL Jong and scientific information to earth.

Japan assured that the primary goal of North Korea was to test the ability to develop a long-range missile in which subsequently it would be placed a nuclear warhead. The president of the United States, Barack Obama, reacted strongly against this and considered it a provocation that must be answered by the international community. But Russia and China called for calm and announced that they would prevent any sanctions to North Korea in the Security Council of the

UN if the United States, France and the United Kingdom --- the three other Security Council members, --- try to pass a penalty.

The attitude of North Korea put the world in a very delicate situation; one can say in a situation on the brink of war. The chronology of the fact was the following:

On February 3, 2009 South Korea announced that North Korea was preparing the test of a missile Taepon 2, able to reach the continental territory of the United States.

Three weeks after, North Korea confirmed the information but in an ambiguous form.

Indeed, on February 24, 2009, the official news agency announced in a statement that North Korea was preparing the launching of a rocket to set in orbit a satellite of communications. Some experts considered that the hide objective was to rehearse a ballistic missile. The true is that the technologies for setting in orbit a satellite would have the same objective because it would permit this country to build rockets of long range.

On March 1, 2009 North Korea accused South Korea of making military maneuvers in its border and warned about unforeseeable conflicts. Previously, on January 31 2009 Pyongyang announced the decision of cancelling the non-confrontation agreements signed with South Korea for the diminishment of the military threat in the Peninsula.

The Committee for the Pacific Reunification of Korea, a North Korean organism, assured that there is no form to improve the relations, because the politics and military confrontations between the two countries have reached a level that set the relations at the brink of war, said a report of EFE-Reuters, from Seoul.

Only two years before, on February 13, 2007 North Korea signed an Agreement with the United States, China, Russia, South Korea and Japan for the dismantlement of their nuclear facilities in exchange of petroleum and new relations with Washington, among other conditions.

Along the year 2008 North Korea used its diplomatic capacity for obtaining advantages but without fulfilling the Agreement of February 2008.

This was not the first time that North Korea did not honor its commitments. North Korea made the same in regard to a similar Agreement signed in the year 1994.

A delicate situation is also happening with Iran, which is developing a nuclear program that will allow this country the construction of nuclear weapons.

Iran assures that its nuclear program is exclusively for peaceful objectives but other countries have doubts about this. Some observers believe that moreover peaceful goals Iran has the intention of building a deterrent nuclear force.

The same day on February 3, 2009 that North Korea announced the testing of the Taepo 2 missile Iran settled in orbit its first self-constructed satellite to commemorate the 30th anniversary of the Islamic Revolution. The Iranian television transmitted the ceremony of the launching. This fact confirmed that Iran owns the technology for building ballistic intercontinental missiles.

It is not a casualty that these two issues have been announced the same day.

North Korea and Iran work together in military affairs. This appreciation is confirmed by the following information of AP on March 29, 2009. The news says that:

"Tokyo's Sankei newspaper said in a separate dispatch from Washington that 15 personnel from the Iranian satellite and missile development company Said Hemmat Industrial Group was staying in North Korea at the invitation of the North Korean government.

Quoting unnamed intelligence sources in Washington it said are close to North Korean affairs, Sankei said the Iranians are likely to join North Korean preparations for the launch and also observe it. The report said North Korea sent missile experts to Iran when it launched a satellite in February.

North Korea is believed to have sold missiles to Iran, and Iran's Safir-Omid space launch vehicle owes much to the North's Taepodong missile."

The great problem is that behind North Korea an Iran is the hand of other nuclear powers of the world, China and Russia.

Without China's help North Korea had not been able to mature its nuclear program.

The same happen with Iran that has received all the support of Russia for the construction of its atomic infrastructure.

These situations put in evidence that there is a double discourse of the great nuclear powers that, on one hand speak about peace but on the other side give nuclear technology to nations as North Korea and Iran that maintain a strong confrontation with the United States.

Which is the true purpose of China and Russia?

Which is the situation of the other powers?

Is the supremacy of the United States in peril?

Which are the politics, economic, environmental and military scenarios and its influence over the world peace?

These are some of the questions that we will try to respond with the intention that you, the reader, can obtain your own conclusions.

This work is divided in two parts; in the first part a vision of the main challenges of the 21st century and its perspectives is presented and in the second part the historic facts related to the natural resources crisis and their consequences are considered.

For the year 2015 the Council on Foreign Relations defined 10 top conflicts:

- The intensification of the conflict in Iraq
- A large-scale attack on the U.S. homeland or ally
- Cyber attack on U.S. critical infrastructure
- A severe North Korea crisis
- The renewed threat of Israeli military strikes against Iran
- An armed confrontation in the South China Sea
- The escalation of the Syrian civil war
- Rising violence and instability in Afghanistan
- Increased fighting in eastern Ukraine
- Heightened Israeli-Palestinian tensions

http://www.cfr.org/peace-conflict-and-human-rights/preventive-priorities-survey-2015/p33990

We agree with that appreciation of the CFR but we add the following:

- Tensions for the water crisis in some regions of the world
- The lack of food in some places of Africa and Asia
- The energy scarcity in some countries

Finally in this introduction I want to say that for a better understanding of this work and to ensure its consistency I had to repeat some ideas on some parts of the document.

First part
The 21st Century challenges

Chapter 1

Effects of the economic crisis on the world stability

The link between economy and politics is beyond doubt. There is a relation of causality between both. In the history of humanity this relation is clearly visible. The trend to violence increases in periods of economic crisis, poverty and unemployment and vice verse, the trend to peace increases in times of prosperity. For example, the two great confrontations of the 20 century, the First World War 1914-1918 and the Second World War 1938-1945 was preceded by a period of severe economic crisis and it may be assured that the two phenomenon's were essentially a consequence of the economic situation.

The economic ruin fed the animosity feelings of the countries and created radical leaders as Benito Mussolini and Adolf Hitler that incited to the war.

Other local conflicts of the 20-century had the same origin: poverty, unemployment and the struggle for the resources.

The 21st century is not an exception and surely the rule of history will repeat again.

For that reason the comprehension of the economic reality is something very important, because it let us anticipate what would happen in the world political scenario.

Two decisive facts dominate the global economic situation: the financial collapse and the natural resources crisis. Both phenomena are closely joined and will determine the political future of humanity, especially war and peace between nations as will be shown in the following pages. For that reason the comprehension of the economic reality is something very important, because it let us anticipate what would happen in the world political scenario.

This information of Reuters on February 12, 2009 reveals the situation:

"World economic crisis is top security threat: U.S. Intelligence

By Randall Mikkelsen– 1 hr 41 mins ago

WASHINGTON (Reuters) – The global economic crisis has become the biggest near-term U.S. security concern, sowing instability in a quarter of the world's countries and threatening destructive trade wars, U.S. intelligence agencies reported on Thursday.

"The financial crisis and global recession are likely to produce a wave of economic crises in emerging market nations over the next year," said the report. A wave of "destructive protectionism" was possible as countries find they cannot export their way out of the slump.

"Time is our greatest threat. The longer it takes for the recovery to begin, the greater the likelihood of serious damage to U.S. strategic interests," the report said.

The report represents the findings of all 16 U.S. intelligence agencies and serves as a leading security reference for policymakers and Congress. Besides reviewing adversaries, it also considered this year the security impact of issues including climate change and the economy.

It said a quarter of countries have already experienced at least "low-level" instability, such as government changes, linked to the economy.

There have been anti-government protests in Europe and the former Soviet Union, and growing economic strains in Africa and Latin America, the national intelligence director, Adm. Dennis Blair, told Congress in delivering the report.

"Instability can loosen the fragile hold that many developing countries have on law and order, which can spill out in dangerous ways to the international community," Blair told the Senate Intelligence Committee.

Steps such as devaluations, tariffs and export subsidies were possible from countries desperate to boost economies."

The report is enough illustrative and do not require more explanations.

The mortgages was not the main cause of the financial fallout

The mortgages crisis was one but not the principal cause of the financial bankruptcy in 2008. The main cause was the economic system itself that put the financial economy in first place.

The priority for the system is the financial speculation and not the production in the real economy. Money is the Supreme God of the system. Nothing is more important than money and everybody invest its money with the hope of obtaining big profits.

The speculation in the Stocks Markets is, then, the other cause of the financial crisis. Bad investments, over appreciation of shares and the fall of the markets were visible some months before the 2008 crisis explosion. The United States Stock Market crisis was the prelude of the banking fallout. [1]

After months of continuous increase, on July 11 2008 the oil reached its maximum historic level, US $ 147; a similar trend was observed in the food prices. The speculators that made huge investments with the objective of obtaining huge benefits caused the explosion of the commodities prices.

These facts contributed to accelerate the financial problems. The first consequence of the commodities price enhance was the reduction of the consumption. The crisis favored some sectors of the economy in detriment of others.

The truth is that the financial crisis came up because the banks had problems hanging over them for many years and not only because of the mortgages situation. A financial crisis of this magnitude does not emerge by surprise.

In financial crisis, bankers save their personal fortunes.

The responsibility for the crisis should be attributed to the directors of the banks that are unable to guarantee the health of the institutions; and on the contrary, act for his own benefit. But the major responsibility is of the countries´ governments that do not exert an effective control on the banks activities.

The year 2008 was not the first time that the financial system collapses and sure it will not be the last. Meanwhile, the public funds ---in other words, the taxpayers--- pay the account for the banker's happiness.[2]

From its birth, capitalism created great crisis

The financial capitalism has dominated the world economy from the last decade of 19th century until the first decades of the 21st century, approximately 120 years. Throughout that time, the financial capitalism accumulated a huge amount of money to build the modern world but simultaneously it has generated major crisis and damage for millions of people and thousands of businesses around the world that have lost their heritage as a result of its speculative practices. For example, "during the period following the First World War the U.S. banks showed a tendency to abandon the field of real banking business and becoming agents of financial speculation. Instead of extending loans, commercial banks used their short-term deposits to buy long period bonds recommended by the major banks and to buy or sell securities to the public willing to invest their money." [3]

Through the so-called "controlled companies" financial capitalism appropriated full productive sectors from where all its actions were executed.

In the twenties led by the voracious American financial capitalism even lowered the wages of the workers to obtain more benefits that, among other errors, destroyed the purchasing power of workers and pushed the country towards the Great Depression.

"From 1920 to 1932 approximately 11,000 banks closed in United

States before the "total closure" which occurred in early March 1933. Only 18,800 banks remained open. There is a contrast between the 11,000 banks, which broke in the United States, which occurred, in the same period in Canada, where only one bank was broken, Home of the Bank in 1932. Meanwhile in United States by 1920 there were about 30,000 banks, Canada only had 10 banks with about 3970 branches." [4]

As it can be seen in the quotations above, the financial capitalism led Capitalism system to its first big failure.

How the American society overcame the Great Depression of 1929

Theoretically one could say that the 1929 crisis was caused in United States for two main reasons: a) the greed of bankers and b) the indifference, the "leisser faire" by the government, which created the conditions for the collapse of the economy. It was a misunderstood economic freedom that put the capitalist system near its end. Through a political action by the government of President Franklyn D. Roosevelt, the United States was able to overcome its most serious economic disruption.

These actions were not only economic but also a political concept known as "The New Deal" in which the state intervention was the main issue.

The first thing President Roosevelt did to address the crisis was --- under strict control of the government --- to reopen the financial system, which had closed its doors in March 1933. Through a stringent law prevented the continuation of the speculation in the stock market, put limits on the excesses of the electricity industry, which had been associated with the predatory practices of financial capitalism; enacted the National Industrial Recovery Act to encourage industry, reorganized the transportation, created the Federal Emergency Relief Administration to provide direct employment to the unemployed, created the Federal Surplus Relief Corporation in October 1933 to provide food, clothing and fuel to the unemployed, began a comprehensive public works program to provide direct employment to workers, revalued the dollar; and through the Home Owners Refinancing Act of June 1933, prevented the seizure of million people who could not pay their mortgages, among other important actions.

History repeats itself and in the years 2008 and 2009, President Barack Obama took a set of measures similar to those adopted by President Franklyn Roosevelt in the thirties of the twentieth century.

Origin of the Global economic failure 2008

In the decade of the eighties in the 20th century appeared in the horizon a new crisis; this affected the majority of countries. In those years the mistakes of the global financial system began to be appreciated; in the precedent decade ---the seventies--- the financial international system gave loans of billions of dollars to the undeveloped countries at usury rates of interest.

The global crisis began when in the eighties the undeveloped countries could not pay their debts. In that moment the financial system employed its power and influence over the governments of the richest countries to impose a new method for recovering the loans and to avoid bankruptcy.

The method was a new system of political economy that was named Globalization. Globalization is a system based in the principles of the Neo liberalism. The main objective of the new economic system was to impede the banks bankruptcy and to improve their benefits.

Bankers were aware that the debt was not recoverable but they created a formula for maintaining the debt as healthy assets. The formula was very simple: the refinancing of debts at perpetuity, changing papers by other papers when these expire. Another formula employed by the financial system has been to issue billons of shares and bonds to be negotiated in the world Stocks Markets. The majority of these shares and bonds are a great risk because are overvalued or do not have any value because do not have any support.

This has been the procedure used by the financial system and the cause of the main crisis of the 20th century as the Great Depression of the thirties and the economic disaster of the first years of the 21st century.

In the eighties, the Globalization and the Neo liberalism was adopted as an official policy by the government of Margaret Thatcher in the United Kingdom and Ronald Reagan in the United States, and it was imposed to the rest of the world through the World Bank and the International Monetary Fund.

The mechanism was simple: the World Bank and the International Monetary Fund dictated a series of conditions to the undeveloped countries: a) adoption of the free market policies b) none intervention of the States in the economy c) privatization of the more profitable public companies to be sold to the international capitals.

These conditions were imposed to the undeveloped countries under threat. The country that did not accept the conditions would not receive new loans of the international financial system and their debts would not be refinanced.

Of course, all the undeveloped nations accepted the conditions because they had no other option.

Political consequences of Globalization

The results of Globalization were not the best. The process of Globalization was a failure. As a consequence of its imposition, the political panorama of many regions of the world changed.

In many countries the governments that adopted the Globalization model fell. In other countries leftist governments emerged. Latin America is perhaps the best example. From the decade of the eighties, 10 Latin American countries have leftist governments.

The establishment of leftist governments in Latin America is a direct consequence of the Globalization and the Neo liberalism policies.

In the first decade of the 21st century the countries with left-wing governments are: Argentina, Brazil, Bolivia, Paraguay, Ecuador, Venezuela, Dominica Island, Cuba, El Salvador and Nicaragua.

But the situation of Mexico must be considered, where a leftist candidate ---Andrés Manuel Lopez Obrador--- lost the election in 2006 by very few votes and where there is a strong leftist movement with an important parliamentary force. This means that Mexico might fall in the hands of the left wing. The same is happening in another country of Central America, El Salvador, where the Political arm of the former guerrilla, the "Frente Farabundo Martí", in January 2009 won the parliamentary elections. In March 2009, the former guerrilla won the Presidency of that country, through Mauricio Funes.

It is necessary to highlight that Brazil and Mexico are between the major's economies of the world. The Globalization and the Neo liberalism ---and especially the financial speculation that is the origin of the poverty of millions of persons worldwide--- also leaded these countries towards the left.

These facts have been a blow for the international policy of the United States.

The banker's avarice provoked the 2008 economic disaster

The financial system sells the idea that you can obtain a lot of money through the financial speculation and in part this is true. If you know the business you can obtain a lot of money through the financial speculation but it is also true that you can lose your investment.

The global economy debacle of 2008 had its origin in the United States financial system. The financial speculation ---banker's avarice--- was the principal responsible of the crisis.

Moreover, there is another important fact that has not been recognized until now; that fact is that the developed nations markets cannot continue growing enough to guarantee the net accumulation of capital in those countries.

The developed economies have reached a saturation level due to the satisfaction of the needs of the majority of the traditional population.

In the case of the United States, the necessities of the recent arrived immigrant are one of the forces that feed the demand in the economy.

In contrast, the majority of the North American people, the native people, have a high level of live in comparison to the level of life of people of undeveloped countries.

The same happens in the other emblematic developed capitalist nations. In the Nordic countries, for example, the level of life is something exceptional.

As a consequence of this situation, in the developed nations the markets work especially for the maintenance; the priority is the reposition investment and not the net accumulation of capital because the internal markets have a limit determined by the satisfaction of the necessities of the majority of the population. A family cannot have 10 cars, 10 refrigerators, and 10 televisions. The demand has a limit because when you reach the satisfaction of all your necessities you usually do not continue buying goods that you have in abundance.

The solution for this problem of the market saturation of the developed countries is in the market of the undeveloped countries towards where the developed economies might channel their exports efforts. The problem is that the undeveloped countries are completely indebted and cannot expand their imports. For that reason the solution of the economic crisis is like the story of the egg and the chicken; what was first, the egg or the chicken?

For resolve this problem it is necessary to create a new international economic policy to expand the consumption ---especially in the undeveloped nations--- that is the great market because of the unsatisfied needs of it population. This implies to review essential issues as de external debt policy and the international commercial treatments.

If you provoke a crisis you cannot solve it

The people that caused the financial fallout are not able to resolve the problem; on the contrary, they make the issue worse.

If you provoke a crisis it is obvious that you did it for two reasons: a) because you were aware and you did it with intention or b) because you were not able to avoid it. As a consequence, in any case, you are not the appropriate person to fix the crisis. The bankers cannot solve the financial crisis, for a simple reason: they provoked it. The governments make a great mistake giving money to the bankers. This appreciation has been sufficiently proven in history. For example, during the Great Depression in the thirties, President Hebert Hoover (1929-1933) committed the huge error of giving financial assistance directly to the bankers. The results were the worse: most bankers took the money for themselves, for their own fortunes, and the population received nothing. That is a lesson in history not only for the United States but also for other countries.

The unique manner of recover an economy after a financial disaster is giving the financial help of the government direct to the consumers and generating public jobs directly. The public investment acts as a locomotive that carry the freight wagons connected to it including the private investment.

The President Obama's government was aware of this situation and on March 3, 2009 made this announce:

Fed launches $200B program to spur consumer loans
By JEANNINE AVERSA, AP Economics Writer 5 mins ago

March 3, 2009

WASHINGTON – The government launched a much-awaited program Tuesday to spur lending for autos, education, credit cards and other consumer loans by providing up to $200 billion in financing to investors to buy up the debt.

If the program succeeds, it should help bust through the credit clogs in place since last year and make it easier for Americans to finance large and small purchases at lower rates, Federal Reserve Chairman Ben Bernanke told Congress. That, in turn, would help revive the economy, he said.

Created by the Fed and the Treasury Department, the program has the potential to generate up to $1 trillion of lending for businesses and households, the government said. It will be expanded to include commercial real estate, though that won't be part of the initial rollout.

"There's a looming crisis in commercial real estate whereby owners of shopping malls, hotels, rental properties and many other types of buildings are unable to refinance or to pay for new construction because the (commercial) securitization market is completely shut down," Bernanke said during an appearance before the Senate Budget Committee.

The program will start off by providing $200 billion in loans to investors with the goal of jump-starting lending to consumers and small businesses. The program, dubbed the Term Asset-Backed Securities Loan Facility, was first announced late last year and originally was scheduled to start in February.

Participants — companies and investors that pledge eligible collateral to back the loan — must request the new government loans by March 17. The Fed will provide the three-year loans on March 25.

"We should see immediate benefits to students, to credit cards, to small businesses, to consumer loans," Bernanke told lawmakers.

Under the program, the Fed will buy securities backed by different types of debt, including credit card, auto, student and small business loans. The credit crunch — the worst since the 1930s — has made it much harder for people to obtain such financing, and those that do can be socked with high rates.

Before the financial crisis, banks relied on packaging such loans into securities and selling them to pay for additional lending. That process had financed about 25 percent of consumer loans in recent years until the credit markets ground to a halt in October, the government said.

Anil Kashyap, a professor at the University of Chicago's Booth School of Business, said the program should make it easier for consumers to get loans. But he cautioned that the Fed's involvement in this area could have unintended consequences elsewhere by making other debt securities not backed by the government less attractive to investors.

"We'd really rather the credit markets just work properly," Kashyap said.

The Fed plans to keep the program running through December, but said it could be extended.

The Fed and Treasury expect that securities backed by car-fleet leases as well as by certain equipment, including for heavy construction and for agriculture, will be eligible for Fed funding in its April operation. Participants in the second round of funding must request the government loans by April 7, which the Fed will disburse on April 14.

The program, the Fed said, would remain focused on securities that are best able to aid the economy and financial markets and that can be added at a low risk to the government.

Limits on executive compensation that apply to financial institutions receiving capital from the $700 billion rescue program won't apply to lenders and other participants benefiting from the program. That's because it wants "to encourage market participants to stimulate credit formation" and use the program, the Fed said.

—

AP Economics Writer Christopher S. Rugaber contributed to this report.

The government of the President Franklyn D. Roosevelt in October of 1933 adopted a similar measure. This was an essential action for recovery the economy those years. In 2009, President Barack Obama's government uses the same policy.

Intervention of the State

United States and Western Europe found a road to fix the economic crisis of 2008: the State intervention.

The States, the governments, paid the mistakes of Globalization and free market.

Leaders of the private sector ---the real leaders of the free market--- have requested the intervention of the States and governments. And the governments and parliaments have given the money especially for the banker's happiness.

The bailout 2008-2009 received too many criticisms in the United States. Diverse complaints on the improper exercise of the financial assistance of the government was revealed by the media, from the use of the resources for investments in the super bowl to the payment of great amount of money ---from the bailout--- to the chiefs of the broken banks.

Meanwhile, the workers of the banks and the savers were the victims; the formers, because they lost their jobs and the second ones because they had to wait the action of the government to get their money back.

The financial system is designed with the purpose of giving all the advantages to the bankers. If the banks fall, the bankers do not lose their money, they keep their personal fortunes and the governments assume the loss.

The banker's avarice was sufficiently demonstrated in the 2008 crisis. The following article published on February 12 2009 by the New York Times confirms it:

Nearly 700 at Merrill in Million-Dollar Club

By MICHAEL J. de la MERCED and LOUISE STORY
Published: February 11, 2009

For nearly 700 lucky Merrill Lynch employees, 2008 was a million-dollar year, even though the brokerage firm lost $27 billion.

On a day the chief executives of eight large banks were questioned about their industry's excesses on Capitol Hill, Andrew M. Cuomo, the attorney general of New York State, raised hackles by disclosing how Merrill Lynch distributed its $3.6 billion 2008 bonus pool. The payments, made just before Merrill Lynch was sold to Bank of America in December, have already stirred anger for being paid earlier than usual. And Mr. Cuomo made it clear that the bulk of the bonuses were paid to a small portion of Merrill Lynch's 39,000 employees.

"Merrill chose to make millionaires out of a select group of 700 employees," Mr. Cuomo wrote in the letter, which was sent to the House Financial Services Committee on Tuesday night.

The disclosure again puts Wall Street's compensation system, which has long rewarded select individuals with handsome bonuses, under the microscope.

Many of the questions at Wednesday's hearing in Washington centered on whether banking chiefs would take bonuses, and Mr. Cuomo has homed in on the payments made to executives by banks that have received more than $350 billion from the federal government. That banks have collectively lost hundreds of billions of dollars has only fueled public scorn.

The Merrill Lynch payments were not alone in the glare. Plans to pay brokers at the new joint venture between Morgan Stanley and the Smith Barney unit of Citigroup have endured a closer look in recent days, especially after a senior Morgan Stanley executive admonished his employees to call the payments "retention awards," not bonuses.

Mr. Cuomo and others have criticized Merrill for moving up the bonus payments to December, just before shareholders approved the merger, instead of the usual time in January. John A. Thain, who as Merrill's chief executive helped orchestrate the firm's sale to Bank of America, was ousted from the combined company last month, largely over the bonus controversy.

For its part, Bank of America has acknowledged that it was fully aware of the amounts and timing. In fact, the bank persuaded Merrill Lynch to reduce the size of the bonuses. But in a statement Wednesday, the bank said: "Although we had a right of consultation, it was their ultimate decision to make." However, several people involved say the bank signed off on the bonuses.

As part of his investigation into the matter, Mr. Cuomo has subpoenaed several executives from both Merrill and Bank of America, including Mr. Thain and J. Steele Alphin, Bank of America's chief administrative officer. Kenneth D. Lewis, Bank of America's chief executive, is likely to receive a subpoena as well.

If that $3.6 billion had been evenly disbursed among Merrill's work force each person would have received about $91,000. Instead, the top four bonus recipients received a total of $121 million, Mr. Cuomo wrote.

One of them was Thomas K. Montag, who now runs global markets at Bank of America, according to a person with knowledge of the matter. Mr. Montag was given a contract worth $39 million when he moved to Merrill from Goldman Sachs last year.

Another was Peter S. Kraus, a former Merrill executive vice president and now the chief executive of AllianceBernstein. The other two were part of Merrill's upper management, this person said.

Other top Merrill executives, including Mr. Thain; Gregory J. Fleming, its former president; and Robert D. McCann, its former wealth management chief, did not receive bonuses.

Mr. Cuomo also wrote that 20 people were paid more than $8 million and 53 people were paid more than $5 million. Some of the bonuses — 30 percent — were paid in stock, according to people with knowledge of the matter.

It is not clear whether Mr. Cuomo will seek to claw back those bonuses. Proving that the payments violated New York's so-called fraudulent conveyance law, which enables creditors to sue to recover unjustified compensation in certain cases, would be difficult because of high legal hurdles. Mr. Cuomo may try to show that Merrill and Bank of America failed to disclose material information about Merrill's financial health to allow the payments to be made.

Separately, the issue of retention payments to brokers of the soon-to-be-combined Morgan Stanley and Smith Barney took on more attention on Wednesday, after the Huffington Post Web site posted audio of a conference call held by James P. Gorman, a Morgan Stanley co-president.

On the call, Mr. Gorman emphasized that the payments were not bonuses, but were a normal award to keep highly prized financial advisers after mergers of brokerage firms. The awards would also be based on the 2008 performances of brokers, not 2009's performance.

Bank of America had also granted generous payments to Merrill's top producing brokers.

James Wiggins, a Morgan Stanley spokesman, said that such payments were necessary and would come out of operating revenue, not government bailout funds. Morgan Stanley has received $10 billion, while Citigroup has received $50 billion.

"We are getting very heavily, aggressively recruited against," he said. "It is important that we retain as many of our successful financial advisers as we can."

Morgan Stanley was contacted by Mr. Cuomo's office last week to discuss the potential retention payments, a person with knowledge of the matter said.

The AIG case

Some weeks after receiving $ 170 billion dollars in government bailout a selected group of approximately 400 AIG employees received bonuses between $ 1,000 and $ 6.5 million dollars.

This means that AIG used the public funds to give gifts to a privileged group of executives instead of using the bailout for fulfilling the true commitments of the company.

Public System

In reality, the intervention of the state by means of the bailout to the banks has become the private financial system in a public system.

Now, the state ---and not the private sector--- is the true owner of a good part of the financial system in each one of the countries affected by the crisis.

Until what point will the states use their power over the banks and will respect the private interests is the great question.

The 2008 crisis demonstrated that the lack of control and supervision by the Government was one of the main causes of the fallout.

Will this change? Will the governments exert a major control over the financial system? The answers to those questions will be a key for the economic future of the world.

The financial system is something essential for all the societies but the reality demonstrates that a severe control of the governments is necessary to guarantee that the system fulfills the commitments in order to have economic prosperity.

Why Communism did not survive

Capitalism survived because it was able of adopting radical measures taken from its ideological antagonist: Socialism; a contradiction itself.

It cannot be denied that the New Deal of President Franklyn D.

Roosevelt during the thirties and forties years of the twentieth century was a combination of liberal and socialist measures that promoted the intervention of the state in the most important social and economic activities of North America. This intervention of the state made possible for Capitalism to survive in this country. If you analyze each one of the policies of the New Deal you will verify that most of them were interventionist policies.

The intervention of the state was the vaccine that saved the Capitalism in the thirties and in the other crisis that this system has suffered since then.

And what is a vaccine?

A vaccine is a product obtained from the same virus that eventually destroys.

Well, Capitalism obtained the vaccine that saved itself from the virus of Socialism; applying Socialist measures in the economy and in the society.

Orthodox Soviets leaders were not able to understand this reality and for that reason the Soviet Union collapsed in the nineties. If the Soviet leaders would have applied the same policy and had used Capitalism measures, perhaps the Soviet Union would have survived. But, on the contrary, they radicalized Communism and the system could not resist. Chinese leaders understood this reality many years ago, and after Mao Tse Tung death in the seventies they applied a new method to guarantee the survival of their communist system. The Chinese leaders have applied the Contradictory Method that their Soviet colleagues were not able to accomplish. China is formally a Communist country but with liberal economic institutions open to the global economy and this has preserved the Chinese regime. How is this contradiction possible?

Theoretically it is not possible but in the reality it works. This demonstrates that sometimes there is a great difference between theory and reality.

The effect of this contradiction that occurs in the reality deserves to be deeply studied by politicians and economists worldwide.

The essence of Capitalism might change

The financial system is the core of Capitalism. Money is the Supreme God of the system. The wealth is the money and not the material resources that stay in second place. This is the cause of the crisis and also the way to solve the crisis. Capitalism fixes all its problems through a formula: the creation of money. With money you can buy anything. Everybody accepts money. But ---the evolution of the facts during the last years--- are demonstrating that perhaps those concepts ---that are the essence of Capitalism--- might change at mid term because of a new reality: the natural resources crisis.

Water, food and conventional petroleum have begun to be scarce goods and during the crisis 2008 emerged signs that confirmed that trend.

By the year 2008 the price of those vital goods reached unbelievable averages and this contributed to accelerate the global recession. There is, then, a direct relation between the commodities price increase and the recession as was demonstrated during 2008.

The availability or the scarcity of the natural resources will have an expression in their prices. Nevertheless, might arrive a moment when money would not be enough for buying the scarce goods. In history there have been moments like these before. For example, during the Second World War, for people in Europe a small amount of salt, a potato, or a piece of bread had no price. Money had no value. True wealth was the food and the peasant was the richest. I know it because I had the testimony of European persons that lived that reality.

Will these situations repeat again?

If the financial system continues their failure and the economies continue their disdain for the real economy, the radicalization of the economic crisis might be a reality in the future, changing the essence of capitalism.

Capitalism will survive because its leaders resort to socialism measures when the system is in peril. The best examples are the policies applied by the governments of the United States and Western Europe ---intervention of the State--- to attack the financial crisis of the years 2008 and 2009.

But, it is possible that in the future the consequences for the capitalist regime would be different: the participation of the State in the rescued companies perhaps will remain creating a new form of Capitalism of State.

The crisis 2008-2009 has demonstrated a new reality: that at long term, the private sector of the economy cannot survive alone without the help of the State.

Other important lesson is that the State, the government has the duty of exert a severe control over the private sector, especially over the financial system.

In the future a free capitalism without the participation and control of the State will not be possible. This fact will represent a total change of the political and economic concepts that have survived so far.

Up to this moment, the lovers of the free market cannot explain and justify their thesis.

The economic failures of the 20th and the 21st century--- have proven that the free market has an insurmountable difficulty: the human being avidity for wealth; therefore, the participation and control of the State is necessary to guarantee the economic development of society.

In practice, because of the bailout, the financial system of the main developed countries is in the hands of the States that have given the necessary money for their survival. This reveals once more the failure of the free market policy.

Many leaders do not want recognize the failure and insist in maintaining the free market policy. But the reality is above all wishes and the truth is evident: the free market concepts cannot be sustained without the support and the help of the States.

The free market is an utopia. Even Adam Smith recognized that from a meeting of merchandisers couldn't result anything different than a conspiracy to enhance the prices.

The avarice of the richest does not have limits. They will always try to get more and more and that is in contradiction with the global wellbeing of society. Therefore, the capitalism system must be reformed and must establish limits to the unlimited accumulation of wealth of some few groups in detrimental of the majority.

The leaders of the twenty most developed countries have recognized this reality and in the Summit of April 2, 2009 they have expressed the necessity of adopting measures to exert a most severe control over the financial system in their countries, among other actions.

Is the supremacy of the United States in peril?

In the last 20 years of the 20th century a deep change began to be visible in the world.

The destruction of the Berlin Wall, the dissolution of the Soviet Union, the intensification of the moral and religious crisis, the increase of the migrations towards the United States and Western Europe, the dominion of the nuclear energy by some undeveloped countries and the natural resources and environment crisis are some of the principal changes experimented by the world in this stage.

The Soviet Union was not the only power affected by the change. Also the United States has changed. Perhaps, the most emblematic change in the United States is its internal politics opening-up allowing that a new young leader as Barack Obama could assume the Presidency in January 2009.

United States is a great country, with an extraordinary population that has played a stellar role in the world. As an example, if the

United States had not participated in the Second World War today neither freedom nor democracy would exist.

United States has contributed in an extraordinary form to the world development and for this reason it has been the first power of the planet, not only from the military point of view but from the political and economic as well.

However, in the last years, there have emerged in the horizon signs that demonstrate that the country might be losing part of its influence and power. The economic crisis of 2008 is one of those cues.

What happens in the United States determines what will happen in the world. For that reason, any change in the United States is important for the rest of the world.

The politics, economic, military and environmental policies of the United States are determinant for the future of humanity in the 21st century.

The Foreign Affairs Policy
New threat to peace
The communist menace was replaced by the Muslim terrorist threat that executed their first intense action on September 11 2000 in New York. From then, the Western World has lived in constant uncertainty.

The reaction to the terrorist act of September 11 was the invasion of Afghanistan and Iraq. But those war acts brought serious consequences for the United States and the Middle East countries.

Iran intensified its nuclear program.

Al-Qaeda terrorist group enhanced its actions in the region and maintains the hostilities in Iraq, Afghanistan and Syria.

Clashes between Jewish and Arabs grew during the last years and the hope of peace seems far away. The war in Gaza in December 2008, January 2009 and 2014 was especially cruel.

Did the US loose the political and military battle in the Middle East? Until January 2009, the United States was not been able to withdraw its troops from Iraq and Afghanistan. On the contrary, it announced that 20,000 new soldiers would be sent to the former country.

To reach peace and have a stable government in Iraq was as a very difficult goal.

The challenge was: if the United States withdraws its forces from Iraq and Afghanistan ---without defeating first Al-Qaeda--- there was a real possibility that this group or other extremist groups take the control of these countries. If this happens, the consequences for the region and the world peace are unpredictable. Sadly, that scenario has occurred and in plenty 2014 extremists Islamic groups develop a bloody war in the entire region.

What to do then?

The hostility towards the US and the Western World in the Middle East countries has been growing in the first years of the 21st century and this represents a major risk for the world peace.

Will Iran develop their nuke?

Without the help of Russia Iran would have not developed their atomic program. As a matter of fact Russia continues helping Iran in nuclear issues. For that reason Iran will achieve its objectives. This demonstrates that the Russian discourse about the control of nuclear weapons is not true.

The sanctions of the United Nations, and the United States and the European Union threat were not enough to stop the Iran nuclear program.

Iran has enough nuclear fuel to make bomb: U.S.

WASHINGTON (Reuters) – The United States believes Iran has stockpiled enough nuclear fuel to make a bomb, U.S. Joint Chiefs of Staff Adm. Mike Mullen said on Sunday.

"We think they do, quite frankly," Mullen said on CNN's "State of the Union" program when asked whether Iran has enough fissile material for a nuclear weapon.

"And Iran having nuclear weapons, I've believed for a long time, is a very very bad outcome -- for the region and for the world," Mullen said.

A watchdog report issued by the International Atomic Energy Agency two weeks ago said Iran had built up a stockpile of nuclear fuel, raising alarm among Western governments that Tehran might have understated by one third how much uranium it has enriched.

The United States suspects Iran of trying to use its nuclear program to build an atomic bomb, but Tehran insists it is purely for the peaceful generation of electricity. Enriched uranium can be used to make nuclear weapons.

U.S. President Barack Obama's administration, which favors diplomatic engagement with Tehran to defuse the dispute over its nuclear intentions, called Iran's nuclear program an "urgent problem" the international community must address.

The IAEA report showed a significant increase in Iran's reported stockpile of low-enriched uranium (LEU) since November to 1,010 kg -- enough, some physicists say, for possible conversion into high-enriched uranium for one bomb.

The IAEA later said Iran was cooperating well with U.N. nuclear inspectors to help ensure it does not again understate the amount of uranium it has enriched, suggesting the uranium accounting shortfall might not have been deliberate evasion.

(Reporting by Anthony Boadle; Editing by Doina Chiacu)

On February 20 2009, a report of AFP informed that the

International Atomic Energy Agency, IAEA, ordered to Iran and Syria to inform about the appearance of non-natural uranium in the Syrian Desert. The IAEA rejected the Damascus's declaration that assured that the uranium particles found in the region of Al Kibar came from the missiles launched by the Israeli Air Force during its strike in September 2007.

United States, Israel and the IAEA have assured that in the Al Kibar region there was a clandestine Syrian nuclear reactor hidden. The IAEA has requested Syria the access to the region but this country has not permitted the inspection.

If this information is confirmed, the conflict in the Middle East will become everyday worse because new countries as Syria would increase the atomic threat in the region. Israel, the other power of the Middle East, has proven that it will do everything to prevent his enemies to get the nuclear power. In a statement in February 7 2009 the Prime Minister, Ehud Olmert, declared that Israel would not tolerate a nuclear Iran. All of the situations mentioned reveal a trend that deserves to be considered in their entire interrelations for a better comprehension of the international reality.

North Korea blackmail to the foreign negotiators

The North Korean negotiators and political leaders of that country have had the ability to blackmail the United States and the other countries that participate in the conversations for the nuclear disarmament.

So far, North Korea has obtained all the requirements in its negotiations with its neighbors and the United States, without fulfilling the commitments made.

The political battle in other parts of the world
Latin America is the other challenge for the United States. In the final decade of the Twentieth century and first decade of the twenty first century the influence of the United States in the region diminished.

The recovery of the influence of the United States of this region will be determined by the political economy that develops in the coming years. To try of impose the free market policy and the Neo liberalism would be a great error that would represent a major cost for the North American foreign policy.

Those policies are not successful in Latin America, because this region has particular characteristics and costumes completely different to the costumes of the developed countries. In Latin America the free market does not exist; monopolies and oligopolies dominate the majority of countries. In the free market system speculation is something common and prices do not descend in conditions of abundance. The laws of the market do not fulfill in the majority of Latin America. The experts of the other countries nor of the international agencies cannot understand this situation. For that reason ---among others--- the globalization and the Neo liberalism was a failure in Latin America.

The main consequence of that failure is that for the year 2009 twelve Latin American countries are governed by Leftist regimes.

Another mistake of the North American policy in Latin America has been to search and to listen the advice of the richest sectors of the region, but these opinions do not reflect the majority of the Continent and that is the other cause of the Neo liberalism failure.

The opinion of important sectors ---as the workers and the intellectuals--- has not been taken in account sufficiently.

Latin America needs to create its own development economic program adapted to its needs and reality.

Another important reflection is in the political field. The political leadership of the United States must realize that carrying out of elections is not enough for considering that a country has a democratic system.

The tyrants also use elections to justify their actions and to keep the power.

China is the new competitor

China is struggling to increase its power and influence in the world and it has the capacity to reach its objective. For example, China is expanding its actions with success especially in Latin America.

On February 21 2009, AP highlighted that in Washington, Jan Shixue, Director of the China's Latin American Institute of the Social Sciences Academy assured that "China wanted to strengthen its relation with Latin America to obtain food and raw materials for a market of 560 million of consumers, and in this way to build a harmonious world, combating the Imperialism and solving the Taiwan problem cooperating to its development."

China's investments in strategic sectors ---as petroleum--- increase worldwide; also the immigration of Chinese citizens towards the rest of the world has increased.

Internal Policy

The US might become a Latin country

This is a metaphor, but something that is not very far from the reality at long term.

In history, the immigration has always exerted a double influence: to receive the culture of the receptor country and to give their culture to the receptor country.

When a minority overpasses the 5 percent of the total population of a country it is no longer a minority but an important part of the inhabitants of that country.

From the political point of view, in a democratic system ---elections--- five per cent of the population is decisive, especially because the difference between candidates is usually small. From the economic point of view it is also very important. For the second decade of the 21st century the Latin population in the US estimated in approximately 10%

Already exist states in the United States with a very important presence of Latin Americans: Florida and California, for example. Even, in the first election of President Bush, the international news agencies highlighted the decisive participation of the minority of Florida's Cubans.

How to resolve the immigration problem is one of the great challenges of the US.

Military Policy
Nuclear security

In the years 2007 and 2008, the international press revealed a chain of facts that exposed how the nuclear security of the United States was suffering a process of weakening.

An important incident happened in 2006, when four electrical fuses for ballistic missile warheads were mistakenly shipped to Taiwan.

The second one was in 2007 when a B-52 bomber was mistakenly armed with six nuclear missiles when it flew between North Dakota and Louisiana bases.

On May 23 2008 occurred other important incident when a fire destroyed part of an underground nuclear launch site in Wyoming.

This kind of facts might reveal that since the Cold War ended, the nuclear powers have diminished their attention on their nuclear security programs.

For example, the following information of the Associated Press published on February 16, 2009 confirms this appreciation:

British, French nuclear subs collide in Atlantic
By DAVID STRINGER, Associated Press Writer David Stringer, Associated Press Writer –

LONDON – Nuclear submarines from Britain and France collided deep in the Atlantic Ocean this month, authorities said Monday in the first acknowledgment of a highly unusual accident that one expert called the gravest in nearly two decades.

Officials said the low-speed crash did not damage the vessels' nuclear reactors or missiles or cause radiation to leak. But anti-nuclear groups said it was still a frightening reminder of the risks posed by submarines prowling the oceans powered by radioactive material and bristling with nuclear weapons.

The first public indication of a mishap came when France reported in a little-noticed Feb. 6 statement that one of its submarine had struck a submerged object — perhaps a shipping container. But confirmation of the accident only came after British media reported it.

France's defense ministry said Monday that the sub Le Triomphant and the HMS Vanguard, the oldest vessel in Britain's nuclear-armed submarine fleet, were on routine patrol when they collided in the Atlantic this month. It did not say exactly when, where or how the accident occurred.

France said that Le Triomphant suffered damage to a sonar dome — where navigation and detection equipment is stored — and limped home to its base on L'Ile Longue on France's western tip. HMS Vanguard returned to a submarine base in Scotland with visible dents and scrapes, the BBC reported.

"The two submarines came into contact at very low speed," Britain's First Sea Lord, Admiral Jonathon Band, said. Band, Britain's most senior naval officer, offered no further explanation.

HMS Vanguard came into service in 1993, has a crew of around 140 and typically carries 16 Lockheed Trident D5 missiles. Under government policy, British nuclear submarines carry a maximum of 48 warheads. At least one of Britain's four submarines is on patrol and ready to fire at any given time.

France's Le Triomphant carries 111 crew and 15 nuclear missiles, according to defense analysis group Jane's.

"This is the most severe incident involving a nuclear submarine since the sinking of the Kursk in 2000 and the first time since the Cold War that two nuclear-armed subs are known to have collided," said Kate Hudson, head of Britain's Campaign for Nuclear Disarmament.

Russia's Kursk nuclear submarine crashed to the bottom of the Barents Sea during a training voyage in August 2000, killing all 118 crew members.

In March 2007 two British sailors were killed in an explosion on board HMS Tireless during a war game beneath the Arctic ice cap. The same submarine crashed into an object, possibly an iceberg, while on patrol in the Arctic in May 2003. And in November 2002 HMS Trafalgar suffered considerable external damage after running aground on rocks off Scotland while taking part in a two-week training exercise

"It's an absolute one in a million chance that the two submarines were in the same place at the same time," said Lee Willett, head of the maritime studies program at the Royal United Services Institute, a London-based military think tank. "There is no precedent of an incident like this — it's a freak accident," he said.

Stephen Saunders, a retired British Royal Navy commodore and the editor of Jane's Fighting Ships, said that while NATO countries let each other know what general area of the Atlantic they are operating in, neither submarine would have had a precise position for the other.

"This really shouldn't have happened at all," Saunders said. "It's a very serious incident, and I find it quite extraordinary."

Both Saunders and Willett said submarines don't always turn on their sonar systems, or make their presence obvious.

"The whole point is to go and hide in a big chunk of ocean and not be found. They tend to go around very slowly and not make much noise," Saunders said.

Willett said the greatest risks from an accident would be from a leak of radioactive waste. An accidental firing of a nuclear weapon as a result of a crash would be impossible, because of the complex processes needed to prime and fire a missile, he said.

Stephane Lhomme, a spokesman for the French anti-nuclear group Sortir du Nucleaire, said his organization is checking the French coastline for evidence of any leak of radioactive material.

"This reminds us that we could have a new catastrophe with a nuclear submarine at any moment," Lhomme said.

———

Associated Press Writers Jennifer Quinn in London and Jamey Keaten and Angela Charlton in Paris contributed to this story.

The nuclear security will be one of the great headaches of the great powers in the coming years because their own systems have begun to present serious failures and because of the incorporation of new members to the atomic club. Undeveloped nations already have the nuclear domain and it is very likely that in the coming years the number of countries enhance. The cases mentioned and the ones to come show the weakness of the nuclear security in different scenarios.

67 computers missing from nuclear weapons lab

By JOAN LOWY, Associated Press Writer Joan Lowy, Associated Press Writer – Thu Feb 12, 1:31 am ET

WASHINGTON – The Los Alamos nuclear weapons laboratory in New Mexico is missing 67 computers, including 13 that were lost or stolen in the past year. Officials say classified information has been lost.

The watchdog group Project on Government Oversight on Wednesday released a memo dated Feb. 3 from the Energy Department's National Nuclear Security Administration outlining the loss of the computers.

Kevin Roark, a spokesman for Los Alamos, on Wednesday confirmed the computers were missing and said the lab was initiating a month-long inventory to account for every computer. He said the computers were a cybersecurity issue because they may contain personal information like names and addresses, but they did not contain any classified information.

Thirteen of the missing computers were lost or stolen in the past 12 months, including three computers that were taken from a scientist's home in Santa Fe, N.M., on Jan. 16, and a BlackBerry belonging to another employee was lost "in a sensitive foreign country," according to the memo and an e-mail from a senior lab manager.

The e-mail was also released by the watchdog group.

The theft of the three computers in January triggered the inventory and a review of the lab's policies regarding home use of government computers, Roark said.

Only one of the three computers stolen from the employee's home was authorized for home use, which raised concerns "as to whether we were fully complying with our own policies for offsite computer usage," he said.

Roark said computers with classified information are "kept completely separate from unclassified computing."

"None of these systems constitute a breach of a classified system," he said.

The e-mail from Los Alamos senior manager Stephen Blair to lab co-workers said the missing computers and Blackberry were "garnering a great deal of attention with senior management as well as (nuclear security administration) representatives."

The security administration memo said the "magnitude of exposure and risk to the laboratory is at best unclear as little data on these losses has been collected or pursued given their treatment as property management issues."

The lab, located in Los Alamos, N.M., employs about 10,000 people

Moral crisis, how the gays gain influence

The developed societies face a severe moral crisis. The recognition of the marriages between persons of the same sex is the cherry of the cake.

The problem is that the gay community requests the right to adopt children. If this is approved ---and please let me use a metaphor--- in very few years the world will be a Gay world, because the children of these couples will not know what is right and normal and what is not. The other problem is that this social group requests to be accepted without restrictions in the armed forces of the countries, and there are politicians that support this ambition of the gay community. This would be the end of the armed forces.

By other hand, the corruption has reached even institutions as the Christian and Anglican churches in several countries, with priests involved in sex scandals with children.

The Energetic Policy Weakness

The United States has an important vulnerability: the petroleum depletion.
Table 1

United States
Oil Production, Reserves and Consumption Years 2000-2005

	Year 2000	Year 2005	% Difference 2000/2005	Year estimated for the oil reserves end
Production *Thousands of Barrels/day*	5,821	5,120	-12	
Reserves *Millions of barrels*	21,765	21,371	-1.8	In 11.40 years 2016 (*)
Consumption *Thousands of barrels/day*	18,656	20,173	8.1	

Source: OPEC Annual Statistical Bulletin 2005 and 2000.

(*) This is the result of dividing the figure of reserves for the year 2005, 21,371 millions of barrels into the figure of the production for the same period, 5,120 thousands of barrels per day, and this result into 365 days. The operation gives as result 11.40 years since the year 2005. This means until the year 2016.

The oil reserves of the United States have not increased. The figures reveal that the country has petroleum for very few years more. For the national security of the United States this is a problem of great magnitude. In reality, the United States will have petroleum hardly up to the year 2016 or some more. In the practice this is nothing, and the essence of the issue is that the entire North American economy, so far, is based in this product. Therefore, in the first years of the second decade of the 21st century, the United States developed a new method for obtaining petroleum: fracking. By mean of this method the United States has augmented its production; but the great question is: can this technology fill the void left by the conventional oil?

Chapter 2

A vital issue

The most important politics and economic issue of the 21st century is the problem of the natural resources availability. This will be the cause of the war and the peace, the cause of the economic progress or of the recession in the coming years.

In the year 2007 we saw diverse politics and economics problems in the first place of the scenario but in the heart of those problems the natural resources are the main cause: the weakness of the dollar front the Euro and other currencies, the real state crisis in the United States, the recession threat in the United States, the confrontation between Iran and the western countries, the agreement between North Korea and its neighbors on the nuclear program, the civil war in Iraq, the confrontation between the United States and Russia by the missiles base in Yugoslavia, the climatic change and the global warming, they are different situations but with a common origin: the natural resources crisis.

The weakness of the dollar front the Euro and other currencies born in the balance of payment deficit of the United States as consequence, among other causes, of the growing imports of oil. The recession threat in the US was a consequence too of the oil price rise, vital commodity that impacts the rest of the prices in the productive chain.

The confrontation between the western countries and Iran is too an energetic confrontation because Iran is the owner of one of the most important petroleum reserves and everyday move away from the western countries. This fact put in danger the oil supply to the western world. On October 17 2007, the President of The United States, George Bush, declared that if Iran develops a nuclear weapon the humanity would face the Third World War.

The North Korea nuclear threat had as main cause the lack of petroleum and food in that country and the cessation of hostilities between the United States, South Korea, Japan, China, Russia and North Korea, are supported in an agreement signed on February 2007 for given petroleum and food to this last country.

The civil war in Iraq is a consequence too of a problem of natural resources. The United States invaded Iraq to assure the petroleum reserves of this country. That is the true.

The confrontation between Russia and the United States by the missiles base in Yugoslavia had as principal cause the struggle by the influence in the Middle East, and since the practice point of view this mean the influence over the oil sources of the region. Russia is diminishing in an accelerated form its petroleum reserves; between the year 2000 and the year 2005 the Russian production of oil passed from 7,459 to 10,942 thousands of barrels per day.

The other international key issues, the climatic change and the global warming, is too a problem of natural resources, because of the effects of these phenomenon on the global environment and the global production of goods and services.

The Natural Resources Crisis

The signs of a natural resources crisis are not yet perceivable for the majority of people in the developed world, but it is a latent process that very soon will be appreciated to global scale. An inhabitant of New York, Washington, London or Paris, possibly does not know what not having water for one or two days per week or for a long period of time is. Probably he doesn't know what electricity restrictions are like; but in other regions of the world these types of limitations are something common or frequent.

Nevertheless, the situation in the developed countries has begun to change and already it exist regions and states in the United States where has been declared the water emergency supply and where also there are problems with the electricity supply.

You, the reader of this essay, perhaps have a doubt and ask yourself if really there is a worldwide crisis of natural resources.

The answer is yes.

Which resources?

There is a crisis of oil, water, food and electricity.

How may be it demonstrated?

The best prove of the natural resources crisis is the price increase of these commodities.

The price of a good reflects the reality of the moment but not the reality of long term.

In the years 2007 and 2008, the evidence of the natural resources crisis was clearer than in other years:

- The oil price surpassed US$ 90 in October 2007 and two month later, on February Tuesday 19 2008, the West Intermediate Texas reached US $ 100.10 in the New York market; on March Monday 3 the price touched US$ 103.95, passing the barrier of April 1980, that adjusted by inflation was for March 2008 US$ 103.76. The race of prices continued on March 2008 and on Monday 13 the West Texas Intermediate went to US$ 107.

  On Friday May 16 2008, the Light Sweet Crude for June delivery reached US $ 126.20 in the New York Market Exchange, and experts assures that the price will ascent toward the US $ 200 for the ends of the year 2008.

- The wheat price and the price of other cereals reached a record;

- The food price in general grew in an important percentage;

- "Over the past five years, municipal water rates have increased an average of 27% in the United States, 32% in the United Kingdom, 45% in Australia, 50% in South Africa and 58% in Canada."[5]

- The electricity price registered the same trend; between the year 1990 and the year 2000 the electricity rates in the United States increased in an average of 5.23% but between the year 2000 and 2005 the enhance average was 26.25%, five hundred per cent more.[6]

Until the first decade of the 21st century, the crisis due to water shortage was limited to specific regions of Latin America, Africa and Asia and has not had a sufficiently important impact to have the attention of the big worldwide mass media nor of the governments of the developed countries. The same has happened with the oil crises, which only have generated increases in the prices of crude and its derivate but without affecting the availability or the supply of these products, except in the 1973 crisis, when the Arab countries decided to suspend their exports towards the United States and other nations of the West.

We can say then, that in spite of the oil crises which have lifted the prices, the inhabitants of the developed nations have always had abundance of derivatives of petroleum, gasoline, diesel, oil, lubricants and other products and this fact has contributed to create the illusion of the existence of infinite reserves, but this is not true.

But the situation of apparent abundance will change very soon as a result of two facts: the overexploitation of the natural resources and the contamination. Water will be the most appreciated good and in second place will be conventional petroleum, since these two resources are every day scarcer, as it can be verified when considering the evolution of the contamination processes, deforestation and blighting at worldwide level and analyzing the behavior of the conventional oil reserves. The pollution increased by the emissions of carbon dioxide and other elements that contribute to the global heating, the extinction of numerous species, the contamination of waters of the seas, rivers and Lagoons and the nuclear tests, among other elements, constitute a serious threat to life.

The aggression to the environment will have an immediate effect and it will be reflected in the reduction of natural resources availability and also in the diminishment of the food supply. At the same time it will also cause an increase of the conflicts among the countries and within the nations.

The intense fight for the natural resources hence will be the main characteristic of the international policy in the next years to come and this will not only generate important geo strategic and geopolitical changes, but also it will be a determinant factor for the war or the peace in the 21st Century.

Other important nations, like China and India, the most populated countries in the world, have in front of them the perspective of a great burden due to the water crisis, while the United States, Mexico, the United Kingdom and Norway, among others countries, will see their conventional petroleum reserves reduced drastically.

This, in general, was the international situation in the first decade of the 21st century. The territorial problems related to the problems of shortage of natural resources, constitute the main cause of the conflicts, as it will be possible to be verified in the pages of this book.

*China is prepared to attack the United States with nuclear
weapons*

My experience as a political analyst tells me that many times the
most important news are not sufficiently divulged or they are not
published by mass media. I could verify this fact once again on July
16, 2005 when I read small 20 centimeters column news that,
nevertheless, contained the most important geopolitical and strategic
information of the last years. The article was about nothing less than
a declaration of an important general of the Chinese military rank
named Zhu Chenghu, Dean of the National University of Defense of
that country, who assured that China was prepared to attack United
States with nuclear weapons, if this country supports Taiwan in its
ambition of independence.

In an official conference with foreign journalists in Beijing, general
Chengh said that "if the Americans use their missiles and direct their
bombs against Chinese territory, China will respond with atomic
arms" and assured that "China is prepared for the destruction of all
its cities to the east of Xian, in the middle of the country, but then, of
course, the Americans will have to count on the destruction of
hundreds of their cities by the Chinese." "The logic of the war
imposes that the weakest power must make the maximum effort to
defeat the enemy," stated the general.

This news, which had to generate an intense worldwide reaction, did
not have major repercussion and passed unnoticed for the majority of
mass media of the world, but not for the Chinese government, who
the day after the declaration of general Chenghu hurried to clarify

the situation saying that it was a personal opinion of the official and not the position of the government.

The question that arises from a fact like this is the following: Can a general in service, who in addition is Dean of the University of Defense of China, dare to say in an official press conference with foreign correspondents that his country will attack with nuclear weapons the first world's power?

Two are the possible answers:

a) He did it without the authorization of his superiors, or

b) He did it with the authorization of his superiors.

In the first case, the declaration is doubly serious because it would reveal that there is a serious process of indiscipline in the Armed Forces of China that can have not only internal repercussions but it can affect worldwide peace.

In the second case, the situation is much more worrisome, because it puts in evidence that the Chinese leadership is seriously considering the scene of the atomic war, terrible thing for humanity.

The threat of general Chenghu is something never seen; none of the Soviet leaders and not even Mao Tse Tung in the heat of euphoria of the Cold War dared to threaten with nuclear weapons. Why does general Chenghu made it right in the middle of peacetime? That is an interesting question that must be taken into account by the rest of the countries of the world. It is not only one more simple declaration of an undisciplined general, no; it is something more than that.

The world did not have a previous experience of a threat like the formulated by general Chenghu, except for the one expressed by the chancellor of North Korea in June of year 2003, when he declared that his country would have to construct a nuclear force of dissuasion to defend itself of the United States.

China has the technological capacity to execute a nuclear attack against the United States and so has North Korea. To clear any doubt on its capacity in that sense, North Korea made nuclear tests in October of 2006 which were verified by other countries of the region.

Since the beginning of the 90´s China has been increasing its military expense. On April 2006, the chancellor of Japan, Taro Aso, expressed the preoccupation of his country due to the increase of the military investment of China and said that this is a subject of high security consideration topic in Asia. "It is not clear in what is China using the money of the military expenses and that creates a sensation of threat for the neighbor countries," said the Japanese minister.

Table 2

China. Military Expenditure
In constant US$ 2005

Year	US$ Million
1990	13,200
1991	13,700
1992	16,500
1993	15,300
1994	14,600
1995	15,000
1996	16,600
1997	16,800
1998	19,300
1999	21,600
2000	23,800
2001	28,000
2002	33,100
2003	36,600
2004	40,300
2005	44,300
2006	49,500

Source: Stockholm International Peace Research Institute, SIPI.
http://first.sipri.org/non_first/milex.php

Although is not visible at the first impression because of the economics and commercial interests, in the bottom there is a hard political struggle between China and the United States.

In its annual report 2008, the Defense Department of the United States stated that the Chinese military budget is the double that the one officially declared and it is concentrated in the space development. The Pentagon affirms that in 2007 China spent between 97 and 139 U.S. $ billions against the 45 billions declared. The Pentagon assures that the lack of transparency of China on its military expenses is a risk for the global stability.

In the year 2007 international news agencies revealed other facts that confirm the great risk that the world runs of a nuclear confrontation by error.

Quoting the 2006 Quadrennial Review Report, the Pentagon assure that China "has the greatest potential to compete militarily with the United States and field disruptive military technologies that could over time offset traditional U.S. military advantages."[7]

The 24 Strategies

China always maintained a modesty attitude about its military power and their national strategic objectives.

In the 1990s decade, in an unusual statement, the former Prime Minister, Deng Xiao Ping, expressed his opinion about the China's strategic objectives. The statement, known as "The 24 Character Strategy" does the following recommendation to the Chinese leaders:

"Observe calmly; secure our position; cope with affairs calmly; hide our capacities and bide our time; be good at maintaining a low profile; and never claim leadership."

And during all these years the leaders has accepted the Deng Xiao Ping suggestion; for that reason the general Zhu Chengu menace, already mentioned, is something very important that deserve to be taken in account.

China's military power

China is modernizing their nuclear force with new intercontinental-range missiles, and with medium-range and anti-ship ballistic missiles designed to strike ships at sea, including aircraft carriers.

For the year 2008, the China's strategic forces consisted of 20 silo-based liquid-fueled intercontinental ballistic missiles, capable of reaching the continental territory of the United States; approximately 20 liquid-fueled limited range; between 15-20 intermediate range ballistic missiles, 50 road mobile missile and Jl-1 submarine-launched ballistic missiles.[8]

Moreover of their nuclear capacity, China had an important conventional force: 74 warships, 57 attack submarines, 55 medium and heavy amphibious ships and 49 coastal missile patrol craft; a powerful air force that is upgrading their B-6 bomber fleet with a new long-range cruise missiles and a ground force of 1.25 million of soldiers.

Situation of Iran

On March 13 2008, the military chief of the United States in the Middle East and Central Asia that include Afghanistan and Iraq, Admiral William Fallon, resigned to their position because of a report of Enquire magazine that said that he was resisting for military action against Iran.

The Admiral said that the press reports were wrong but his statement became a distraction that hampers his efforts in the Middle East.

Throughout the time in the press of the United States have appeared many comments on a possible action against Iran. The comments do not assure if is an invasion or an air strike to the nuclear plants but in any scenario, an attack to Iran would provoke a difficult world situation. The first main consequence would be the reduction of the Iran petroleum exports. This fact would impact the prices and would create an important restriction in the availability of this resource affecting the world economy. Moreover, it is necessary highlight that Iran dominate a good part of the Persian Gulf and the Gulf of Oman, key waters through where pass the tankers that comes from Saudi Arabia, Iraq, Kuwait, Qatar, Bahrain, the United Arab Emirates and Oman. This means world chaos because the petroleum transport since the most countries of the Middle East might be affected.

Since the military point of view, an attack would increase the feelings of confrontation in the region and it is very likely that Iran attack to Israel. This country has a powerful military conventional force and the nuclear capacity for responding to an attack.

In the third week of March 2009, the President of United States, Barack Obama, in a message transmitted by the International Voice of America, invited authorities in Iran to improve relations between the two countries and establish a direct dialogue.

The response of the Iranian leadership, led by the religious leader Ayatollah Ali Jameini was a rejection and he assured from the city of Mashad on 21 March 2009 that "United States is a country hated in the world." Far from accepting the offer of the President of the United States, the ayatollah Jameini said that the Iranians "have not perceived any change in the U.S. policy."

This position of the maximum Iranian leader made difficult a diplomatic arrangement of the relationship between United States and Iran. ¿How long will Iran maintain this position? The answer to this question is the key to the future of world peace.

In only thirty minutes the nuclear war can begin

The reliability of the security systems that protect the world of an atomic war is also in doubt. This was confirmed by the Director of the International Atomic Energy Organism, Al Baradei, who when receiving the Nobel prize of Peace on December 10, 2005 in Oslo declared the following: "It is unbelievable that fifteen years after the Cold War the leaders of the nuclear powers, with arsenals prepared in maximum alarm, only have thirty minutes to decide if they respond to an attack."

This is the other great news that had to bring about an intense worldwide reaction but that also happened unnoticed for the majority of the mass media. What the head of the worldwide organism of atomic energy declared is something simply terrible, because of what it means for the life of all the human beings.

That means that the nuclear destruction may occur at any time if anyone of the ones in charge to verify the security of the nuclear systems commits an interpretation error, because there is no time to verify that it is an error.

Thirty minutes is the time that the leaders of the great atomic powers have available to decide if humanity finishes or not, because an atomic war is the end of everything.

What would happen if by an error of the radars or other informatics systems a country like the United States, Russia or China thinks that it is going to be attacked with atomic weapons? What would happen if a high official as General Zhu Chenghu convinces the leadership of his country that there exists an imminent threat of nuclear attack on the part of the United States, Russia or any other country?

The same is applicable to other countries where there are radical people ready to provoke war; therefore the nuclear power has turned the Earth into a highly uncertain scenario with an immense potential of destruction.

Can the Cold War be repeated in the 21st century?

The worldwide situation is getting more complicated because in the first two decades of the 21st century arose once again signs about the possible repetition of the Cold War episodes that were already surpassed after the dissolution of the Soviet Union in 1991.

Indeed, the idea of the United States to place 10 intercepting missiles in Poland and extreme sophisticated radar in the Czech Republic, as part of his protective shield against attacks of probable enemies like Iran and North Korea, found a strong rejection of Russian authorities, who consider the system as a direct attack against their own security.

On October 3, 2006 the spokesman of the Russian State Department, Mijaíl Kamínin, assured that those plans harmed the strategic security of their country. Other Russian spokesmen ratified the opposition to the installation of the shield of missiles and made strong declarations. General Yuri Baluyevski, head of the General Staff of the Russian Army, assured on May 7, 2007 that his country was preparing measures in answer to the installation of the missiles.

Official Soviet sources informed on May 2007 that for the year 2010 Russia would have ready Topol-M ballistic missiles with multiple heads, which are unbeatable even for the strategic shield that was developed by the United States. General Nikolai Solovtsov, commander of the Russian Strategic Forces, informed this.

The Topol-M rockets are considered intelligent rockets with a capacity to carry up to six nuclear heads and are able to destroy targets up to 10,000 kilometers or more of distance. According to the sources they are of fifth generation, and have 22,7meters in length, they weight 47 tons and use a solid propellant.

A View of what the future could be like, can be inferred of the words of the of Russian president, Vladimir Putin, who on February 12, 2007 in the International of Security Conference celebrated in Munich, said that "the United States tries to impose its political system and its ideas to the entire world" and that "the form in which the United States operates often makes difficult a political solution for the crises affecting the world and that is very dangerous." He also he affirmed that his country felt militarily threatened by the United States.

A declaration of this kind made by the maximum Russian authority had not taken place since the Cold War and this is not something positive for the stability of the world.

The declarations of the Chinese general and the Russian generals are worrisome signs and reveal that the world seems to direct itself dangerously towards one-second edition of the Cold War. Together to these potential threats, there are all the situations of confrontation in Iraq, Afghanistan, Syria, Lebanon, Israel and Palestine.

Besides its military power, Russia is one of the great oil producers and in the middle of a crisis of natural resources it could use its petroleum as a political instrument.

Petroleum will have a decisive role in the world peace in the 21st century. The struggle of the main world powers to assure its petroleum provision will intensify in the coming years in the same proportion that the exhaustion of this resource becomes more and more visible. At the same time a fight for the water will be developed, which is scarcer every day in different regions of the world. This is then, the new reality: the accelerated exhaustion and the increasing contamination of important natural resources at a global level.

Chapter 3

Main causes of the crisis

Politics and military causes:
- The government's indifference and the pressure that realize powerful sectors for hidden the true of the environmental damage worldwide
- Nuclear tests and other weapons developments
- Civil wars and the international conflicts, because of the great damage to the productive lands that these events cause.

Economics and demographics causes:
- Natural growth of the world population
- Increase of the effective demand on the Third World and,

especially, in China, India and Latin America

- Diminishment of basic commodities availability and supplies

Environmental causes:
- Overexploitation of land and seas resources,
- Ruin of land: by deforestation, use of pesticides and other toxic materials, bad use of garbage

- Fresh water sources smash

- Contamination of air

- Destruction of the oceans and seas: by petroleum spills, nuclear tests, the garbage deposit in the bottom of the seas

- The climate change and its consequences:

- Global warming, that is attributed by a good part of the experts to the growing use of the fossil fuels

- Melting of the poles and of the glaciers that exists in other parts of the world

- Increase of the natural disasters: floods, droughts, hurricanes and of the levels of the seas, forests fire.

Global oil crisis indicators

The oil reserves are diminishing while the production and consumption grows rapidly. In the table you can appreciate the situation.

Table 3

Crude Oil Production, Reserves and Consumption of Refined Products, Total World 2000-2005.

Years	Production		Reserves		Consumption	
	Thousands of	%	Millions	%	Thousands of	%
	Barrels/day	Change	Barrels	Change	barrels/day	Change
2000	65,824		1,077,499		71,389	
2001	65,392	-0.66	1,085,806	0.77	72,195	1.13
2002	64,046	-2.06	1,121,225	3.26	72,651	0.63
2003	67,283	5.05	1,138,574	1.55	73,981	1.83
2004	70,578	4.90	1,145,125	0.58	76,809	3.82
2005	71,762	1.68	1,153,961	0.77	77,526	0.93
	Average Growth		Average Growth		Average Growth	
	of Production		of Reserves		of Consumption	
	0.17		0.26		1.67	

Source: OPEC Annual Statistical Bulletin 2005 pages 45, 63, and 8; idem 2000.

A report of Exxon Mobil assures that "even with significant improvements in energy efficiency, the world's total energy demand is expected to be approximately 40 percent higher by 2030 than it was in 2005. The vast majority of this demand increase will take place in developing countries."[9]

The International Energy Annual Report 2005 of the United States Government asserts that "World marketed energy consumption is projected to increase by 57 percent from 2004 to 2030. Total energy demand in the non-OECD countries increases by 95 percent, compared with an increase of 24 percent in the OECD countries."[10]

The projections of Exxon Mobil and the Energy Agency of the United States are different but they coincide in the huge growth that the energy demand will have in the future.

But if you consider the situation of the most important petroleum producers of the Western Hemisphere for the year 2005, you check that the crisis is very near.

The following information published by the author on October 29 2008 reveals clearly the situation:

The oil price reduction is temporary and very soon will reach unbelievable levels

The UK oil will last only 4 years more, the USA and Mexico oil only 8 more years.

The abundance of oil is something temporary and the sign of the oil crisis will be visible soon. Now, on October 2008, when the oil price down to less of U.S. $ 100, I am sure that this reduction is something temporary and that the oil price will reach unthinkable levels at medium term.

The United Kingdom will be the first Western country where the oil will finish. If that country maintains the production and the level of reserves that had for the year 2005, the collapse of the United

Kingdom oil will occur in four years, it means, for the year 2012.

A similar phenomenon has already happened. Indeed, on 28 May 2008, an important member of the OPEC, Indonesia, announced their withdrawal of the Organization, because of already do not have enough oil and cannot continue to being an exporter. In Norway the oil will last seven years more, until the year 2015; in the United States and Mexico only eight more years, until the year 2016; in China nine more years, it means, until the year 2017.

Between the year 2000 and the year 2005, the oil reserves of the United Kingdom diminished 19.4%, from 5,002 million of barrels to 4,029 million of barrels. The reserves of Norway presents a similar situation, because passed from 13,158 millions of barrels to 9,691 million of barrels, it means, -26.3%.

The reserves of the United States passed from 21,765 millions of barrels to 21,371 million barrels, 1.8% less.

Mexico's situation is more dramatic because its reserves diminished 48.5% from 28,260 million of barrels to 13,700 millions of barrels.

China presents a similar situation, because their reserves diminished 33% passing from 24,000 million of barrels to 16,038 millions of barrels.

The figures demonstrate the reality. If this trend continues, in very few years the energetic crisis will appear. [11]

On June 3 2014, the U.S. Energy Information Administration confirmed the forecast made by the author Pablo Rafael Gonzalez on October 29 2008 like you can appreciate in the following link:

http://pablorafaelgonzalez.blogspot.com/2014/06/eia-report-confirms-forecast-of-book.html

Oil might be declared patrimony of humanity

The struggle for petroleum will dominate the international politics scenario in the coming years because of a simple reason: oil is running out and the world extracts and consumes more that what is able to restore through the discovery of new reserves.

The oil countries will be, then, the main objective of the non-producers countries. In the described hypothesis is very likely that oil be declared a good patrimony of humanity and not property of any country in particular. This will justify the military intervention of the rest of the world in the petroleum countries. So far this has not happened only for one simple reason: because has been enough petroleum, but when the scarcity be more evident and the supply diminish to critic levels, the law of the strongest will impose.

As is natural, this will generate great conflicts, including the risk of a nuclear limited confrontation.

Fracking, the new technology applied in the second decade of the 21st century will not be enough to satisfy the global requirements of oil.

Indicators of the water crisis

The world water resources are under pressure because of the high population growth, the climatic change and pollution. Already it can be observed that the world run quickly toward the global water crisis.

The earth's hydrological cycle is being modified by the climatic change. The consequence is the reduction of the surface water availability and the groundwater recharge.

The precipitations patterns are the main victims of the climatic change causing severe droughts, floods and hurricanes worldwide. About 40 per cent of the precipitation that falls on land comes from ocean-derived vapor. The remaining 60 per cent come from land-based sources.[12] The global warming is changing the oceans temperatures transforming the weather. By mean of the hydrological cycle the oceans transfers water to the ground and to the plants and since them to the atmosphere. The problem is that this natural process is everyday affected because of the temperature increase.

Only 2.5 per cent of the world water is integrated by freshwater. This means that 97.5 per cent of the world's water belongs to the seas and oceans. 68.7 per cent of the freshwater is located in the glaciers and 30.1 per cent in the groundwater. The surface and atmospheric water –that include freshwater lakes, soil moisture, atmosphere, wetlands, plants and animals-- represents 0.4 per cent of the total water but it provide 80 per cent of the annually renewable surface and groundwater.

By effect of the global warming, the main glaciers of the world – including the poles—are melting. The Himalaya Glaciers are a clear example; they nurture five of the most important rivers of Asia. The same happen in the Alps Glaciers that feed the regional European rivers. The Italy south and the southeastern Europe territories are already affected by the water stress. The glaciers of the Andes regions in South America are also threatened and the evidence is clearly appreciated in Bolivia and Peru. As a consequence of this fact it does not exist water in some regions of those countries and the situation will be worse when the melting of the Andes Glaciers increase.

Thursday 27 of March 2008, the world was surprised by a new disclosed by the international agencies: the information said that an enormous ice block with a surface four times superior to the city of Paris detached from Antarctica.

The gigantic ice block was 41 kilometers of length and 2.5 kilometers of width and separated from the Antarctica Isthmus and continues moving. This ice block was part of the Wilkins platform, which is a floating ice mass of 16,000 square kilometers, that is to say, as large as Northern Ireland.

Scientists have expressed concern because they have discovered that the permanently frozen layer of ice on the colder regions, and including Canada, Alaska, Russia, Northern Europe and Antarctica has begun thaw.

This layer of ice, known as permafrost, contains a large amount of CO_2 and methane, two of the worst gas greenhouse gas emissions (green house). To thaw the permafrost, these gases are released into the atmosphere accelerating global warming. So the situation is truly alarming.

The Centre for Defense Information, one of the most qualified international organisms in this matter explains the consequences of the global warming in the following terms:

"Led by CDI Senior Advisor Philip Coyle, our new project on the international security implications of global climate change aims to study and expand awareness of the many security concerns global warming will create in the near future. For example, if sea levels rise just six meters -- this will happen if the Greenland glaciers melt but nothing more -- 93 million Chinese will be displaced. Massive population displacements due to loss of land mass would be expected elsewhere around the world in India, Bangladesh, Myanmar, the Persian Gulf, Vietnam, Thailand, Indonesia, and the Philippines. Other impacts would include the availability of fresh water, changing growing seasons, and the reach and geographical range of infectious disease. Over the course of the next year, CDI analysts will uncover the many aspects to this issue: including the direct impact on nations; the economic and agricultural impacts; the effect on the U.S. military at home and overseas, and the effects on fuel consumption by the military; as well as mitigation and adaptation options.[13]

In the first years of the 21st century, the signs of water scarcity have appeared in diverse countries and regions, include in the most developed countries as the United States. A very important part of the United States territory --the west, south-west and south-east—is impacted by the water stress and emblematic rivers as the Colorado River is suffering the consequences of the overexploitation of their waters. Some signs reveal the magnitude of the problem. For example, in Georgia, in the year 2007, was declared the water emergency and the water price for the consumers increased 150%. Other states of the US southeast as Alabama, Tennessee, and South Carolina are in the same situation. In the west coast, in California, the water crisis leads to severe restrictions and also the states of the southwest are seriously affected.

Too few countries have increased their water resources available as may be appreciated in the following tables. For example, between the most important developed countries only Russia enhanced its water availability. The United States and Australia was the most affected in the period 2000-2005.

Table 4

Water Availability Information. TARWR* Principal Developed Countries

Country	TARWR per capita 2000	TARWR per capita 2005	2000/2005	% Variation
Australia	25,780		24,710	- 4.15
Canada	94,353		91,420	- 3.10
France	3,439		3,370	- 2.00
Germany	1,878		1,870	- 0.42
Japan	3,383		3,360	- 0.68
Russia	30,980		31,650	2.16
United Kingdom	2,465		2,460	- 0.20
United States	10,837		10,270	- 5.23

Source: AQUASTAT, FAO 2005, 2nd UN World Water Development Report 2006, "Water a shared responsibility", table 4.3 page 132.

* TARWR means Total Actual Renewable Water Resources and is an index that reflects the water resources theoretically available for development from all sources within a country.

The water crisis in the most populated nations, China and India, is already a reality and, as a consequence of this fact, the food production is in danger in those countries. China diminished their water resources availability in -5.27 and India in -6.91 between the year 2000 and the year 2005.

The situation in other countries of the Middle East and Asia is very difficult. Saudi Arabia, the most important petroleum producer of the world have a crisis of water and in the same situation are the other petroleum countries like Bahrain, Iraq, Kuwait, Oman, Qatar and the United Arab Emirates.

The situation in the Palestinian Territories of Gaza and Israel is also complex, as may be verified in the next table.

Table 5
Water Availability Information. TARWR* Selected Countries of the Middle East and Asia

Country	TARWR per capita 2000	TARWR per capita 2005	2000/2005	
Bahrein	181		157	-13.26
China	2,259		2,140	-5.27
Gaza Strip Palestinian Territories	52		41	-21.15
India	1,880		1,750	-6.91
Indonesia	13,381		12,750	-4.72
Iran	1,955		1,970	0.77
Iraq	3,287		2,920	-11.17
Israel	276		250	-9.42
Kuwait	10		8	-20.00
Oman	388		340	-12.37
Qatar	94		86	-8.51
Saudi Arabia	118		96	-18.64
United Arab Emirates	58		46	-20.69

Source: AQUASTAT, FAO 2005, 2nd UN World Water Development Report 2006, "Water a shared responsibility" table 4.3 page 132.

"Our water resources, irregularly distributed in space and time, are under pressure due to major population change and increased demand. Climate change is having a significant impact on weather patterns, precipitation and the hydrological cycle, affecting surface water availability, as well as soil moisture and groundwater recharge. The growing uncertainty of surface water availability and increasing levels of water pollution and water diversions threaten to disrupt social and economic development in many areas as the health of ecosystems."[14]

The situation is not different in America where may be appreciated that the most of the countries suffered an important reduction of their water availability as show the following table.

Table 6
Water Availability Information. TARWR* Selected Countries of America

Country	TARWR per capita 2000	TARWR per capita 2005	2000/2005	% Variation
Argentina	21,980		20,940	-4.73
Brasil	48,314		45,57	-5.68
Chile	60,614		57,640	-4.91
Colombia	50,635		47,470	-6.25
Ecuador	34,161		32,170	-5.83
Guatemala	9,773		8,790	-10.06
Mexico	4,624		4,360	-5.71
Nicaragua	38,787		35,140	-9.40
Peru	74,546		69,390	-6.92
Uruguay	41,654		40,420	-2.96

Source: AQUASTAT, FAO 2005, 2nd UN World Water Development Report 2006, "Water a shared responsibility" table 4.3 page 132.

The forests raze worldwide reinforce the drought trend. The most important forest reserve that still survive, the Amazon region, everyday is devastated by miners and lumberjacks. There are regions in Asia and Africa where already do not exist forests because of the same cause.

"World Resources Institute WRI has estimated that 41 percent of the world's population, or 2.3 billion people, live in river basins under 'water stress,' meaning that per capita water supply is less than 1,700 m³/year (Revenga 2000). Water scarcity is partly due to the uneven geographic distribution of water, as determined by the Earth's climate system.
Water scarcity, whether due to physical, social, or infrastructural reasons, poses significant challenges. The 1.1 billion people without safe drinking water and 2.6 billion people who lack sanitation are particularly at risk for poor health. Globally, nearly 6000 children under the age of five die every day from diarrhea-related diseases (UNICEF/WHO). Water scarcity issues also have relevance for food

production, business, and livelihoods; globally, 70 percent of all water withdrawals are for agricultural purposes and 20 percent are for industrial purposes"[15]

There are other facts that confirm the water crisis that affects the world: Egypt and Ethiopia, for example, are very close to have war conflicts because Egypt has increased its dependency of waters of the Nile River, whereas Ethiopia reduces the river's volume.

The waters of the Panama Canal are losing depth and this puts in danger navigation.

The water-bearings of the border between the United States and Mexico are drying quickly, meanwhile the Ogallala, the most important aquifer of the United States, located between Colorado, Kansas, New Mexico and Texas is too suffering a quickly depletion.

The water-bearings of the western zone of Israel also undergo an intense and constant deterioration and this is one of the main sources of conflict with the Arab population that lives in those territories.

The water availability of freshwater is threatened by other circumstance: the pollution that contaminates the surface water, rivers, lakes and also the groundwater. The discharges of any kind of pollutants elements on the surface water reduce the drinking water availability. These contaminants elements pass to the groundwater and damage the aquifers. This phenomenon is common in the entire world. The contamination of waters comes from the fertilizers and pesticides in the agriculture and from the industrial developments especially.

The facts presented reveal a trend: the diminishment of the water resources and their contamination worldwide. Without water the life is not possible. Man depends of water for drinking, for the agricultural and industrial use, for environment and sanitation proposals. The evidence show that every day there is less available water and the great challenge of the human being in the next years is what to do to survive in a world where the water and other essential natural resources every day are scarcer.

Meanwhile, the great military powers of the world prepare their strategies for scenarios of confrontation because of the water crisis.

Indicators of the food crisis

The behavior of the worldwide cereal stocks is a clear sign of the situation. A report of the Food and Agriculture Organization of the United Nations, FAO, of February 2008 reveals "international wheat prices in January 2008 were 83 per cent up from a year earlier."

The report says that "although prices are high, total world trade in cereals is expected to peak in 2007/08, driven in great part by a sharp rise in demand for coarse grains, especially for feed use in the European Union."

Table 7
World Cereal Stocks, Million Tonnes.

	2003	2004	2005	2006	2007 estimate	2008 forecast
Total Cereal	489.9	417.4	466.7	469.2	419.7	420.2
Wheat	202.5	161.2	176.6	178.5	157.6	143.2
Rice	119.0	105.2	98.9	105.5	106.7	107.0

Source: Food and Agriculture Organization of the United Nations. FAO, Crop Prospects and Food Situation, October 2007. Rome. Table A2.

Other official document of the agency, titled *FAO Food Outlook November 2007*, highlight that "rebounding demand together with tight supplies and rising production costs sustained meat prices in 2007. FAO's meat price index recovered from the low value of 112 in March 2006 to 123 in August 2007 (1998-2000=100), reflecting higher prices for all the three major groups of meat, i.e. bovine, pig and poultry meat. With increased costs of production in major producing countries, the rise in prices can be expected to continue." The report says that despite a slight tendency for pig meat prices to firm over the year, by August 2007 the FAO's pig meat price index stood at only 99 points; up from 96 in August 2006. Much of the growth reflected developments in China where low domestic supplies have converted the country from a net exporter to a net importer." The situation of China deserves to be mentioned because of their impact on the world supply and demand.

The report of FAO recognizes that many countries are victims of food emergencies in Africa and in other regions, like the Near East, Central America and the Caribbean and South America. . "In the Far

East of Asia, a new weather-related emergency has arisen in China."

The report assure that "In China, since 10 January 2008, 14 provinces in the southern and eastern parts of the country have been affected by the most disastrous ice rain, snow and freezing weather since 1951 in terms of geographical extension, intensity and related damage. To the end of January, about 90 million people were reported directly affected and millions of hectares of crops, especially vegetables and oil crops were reported severely damaged. Mongolia is experiencing a particularly harsh winter, which may have a significantly negative impact on livestock. In Bangladesh, emergency food aid continues to be needed for the poor households severely affected by a super cyclonic storm in mid-November, which caused extensive damage and affected some 8.9 million people in 30 districts. The food supply situation for millions of people in the Democratic People's Republic of Korea remains a serious concern as a result reduced crop production and economic constraints. The food security situation in Timor-Leste has been negatively affected by reduced cereal production and rising cereal prices."

After of considering the previous facts and figures, we can conclude that the perspective of the food supply is not the best at medium term. If the climate change continues its progressive intensification, the situation will be worse each day and the food availability will be in a growing danger.

Together with the environmental problem must be taken in account the rising demand in the undeveloped countries and especially the growing demand of China and India that affect the global supply of food and other commodities.

In 2008 the situation arrived to such an extreme that the United Nations World Food Program warned on April 1, 2008 the serious consequences of the increase made on prices of food and assured that the worldwide reserves of food were in the lowest level of the last thirty years.

The rise of prices, assured the agency, is caused by the increase of the prices of fuels, by the growth of the demand in the emergent economies as China and India and by the competition between the space to produce food and the space to produce bio combustibles.

On the other hand, the president of the World Bank, Robert Zoellick, on April 2, 2008, declared that it is necessary to put in practice a new policy in food matters as ambitious as the "new deal" policy developed by the North American president Franklin Roosevelt after the 1929 crisis.

The World Bank considered that 33 countries were threatened with political destabilization and social disorders because of the brutal increase of the prices of agricultural and energetic products. In February 2008, the real price of the rice reached its higher level in 19 years and the price of the flour a record in 28 years, assured the president of the World Bank.

Ministers of the Group of the Eight who met in Tokyo on April 6, 2008 assured that the problem of the rising of the prices of food is something that the international community must consider.

Indicators of the electricity crisis

The electricity scarcity is affecting not only to the undeveloped countries but also to the industrial countries.

Between the year 1996 and the year 2006, the electricity prices in the United States registered an important increase that demonstrates the situation of the supply as may be verified in the following table.

Table 8
United States. Average Retail Prices of Electricity, Cents per Kilowatt Hour Including Taxes, Nominal Prices.

Year	Residential	Commercial	Industrial
1990	7.83	7.34	4.74
1991	8.04	7.53	4.83
1992	8.21	7.66	4.83
1993	8.32	7.74	4.85
1994	8.38	7.73	4.77
1995	8.40	7.69	4.66
1996	8.36	7.64	4.60
1997	8.43	7.59	4.53
1998	8.26	7.41	4.48
1999	8.16	7.26	4.43
2000	8.24	7.43	4.64
2001	8.58	7.92	5.05
2002	8.44	7.89	4.88
2003	8.72	8.03	5.11
2004	8.95	8.17	5.25
2005	9.45	8.67	5.73
2006	10.40	9.36	6.09

Source: Energy Information Administration. Annual Energy Review 2006 table 8.10 page 257.

The United States Department of Energy highlight that more than half of the electricity generated in the United States come from coal and this resource will continue to be the dominant fuel used for electric production because of their low cost and abundance.

The problem is that coal is one of the most generators of pollution. The challenge for the technology is to develop new methods for eliminates the sulphur, nitrogen and mercury released when coal is burned, to avoid the greenhouse gases that contribute to the global warming and to increase the fuel efficiency of coal-fueled power plants. The Department of Energy asserts that today's plants convert only a third of coal's energy potential to electricity. If is improved the efficiency this amount might increase and that means more affordable electricity and fewer greenhouse gases.

In the undeveloped countries the situation is different because they don't have enough financial resources or technological capacity to achieve production and environment protection methods. This represents a true problem for the entire world because the pollutions levels reached until now is unattainable in the time.

Politics and military consequences

The increase of the difference between countries, especially between the United States and the signers of the Kyoto Protocol by the environmental protection is a scenario that has to be considered.

However that the evidence is indubitably, there are powerful sectors -especially of the United States- that deny the natural resources and environmental crisis. These sectors -that come from the petroleum industry especially- have enough influence for determining the United States policy.

The United States contribute with the most part of the pollutants elements that affect the environment, for that reason, its cooperation is vital for the environment protect success.

The main objective of the oil industry is to discover new reserves and to gain access to new petroleum areas in the entire world.

The struggle by the scarce resources will be the principal characteristic of the coming years. The struggle for petroleum, especially, will be intense between the superpowers and the emergent powers as China and India.

China is looking petroleum in all the continents. The United States too. For that reason invaded Iraq in the year 2003. In the measure that the oil scarcity be most, in that same measure will invade other petroleum countries because for the United States oil is a survival issue. The United States petroleum reserves are every day minor, but it consumption is every day superior. Without growing petroleum supply the American economy cannot exist; therefore, the United States will do anything that is necessary to guarantee its oil supply.

Economic and demographic consequences

Moreover of the struggle for petroleum, the world will face a critic situation as a consequence of the food production diminishment. Already may be appreciated the signs of that crisis of the cereals reduction supply and in the proteins production decrease.

The lack of water, and it contrary, severe floods in important regions of the world is a cause of the food production crisis.

China, for example, the most populated country of the world, will battle for food, because of the severe lack of water that threat its agriculture, also India and the countries of the Middle East and

Africa. The immigration of millions of persons since these regions toward the most developed countries will be accentuated in the coming years, in the measure that the crises of natural resources enhance.

The most important economic consequence of the natural resources scarcity is the rise of the food price. This means that the inflation will be present perhaps for much time. The food price increase will affect especially the poor countries that do not have enough currencies to pay its imports.

Effects of the environment damage

In the measure that the environment damages growths the natural resources supply results affected.

The climatic change has altered the weather and the results is the enhance of the number of floods, droughts, hurricanes, the sea level increase, the melting of the poles and of the tropical glaciers.

As a consequence of the predatory man action, a good part of the world forests has been razed. There are regions in Asia and Africa where already there are neither forests nor water. The Amazon region that is the last forest reserve that last in the world is seriously threatened.

The world risk is of such magnitude that the leaders of the most important industrial nations are realizing intense efforts for finding solutions that let diminish the problem; the following report of the World Bank reveals the concern of the world leaders:

"The Japanese Prime Minister Yasuo Fukuda announced on

February 20, 2008 that the sustainable management of forests would be the priority of G8 Summit.

While promoting sustainable forest management, we need to try to halt deforestation and forest degradation, PM Fukuda said at the opening session of the GLOBE Brasilia Legislators Forum. I intend to promote a discussion on forest-related issues with the countries concerned in order to make important progress towards their resolution, Fukuda added.

The Japanese premier also emphasized the importance of address in global warming in his speech, calling it an unrivalled challenge to humanity. He said Japan could contribute by reducing its own greenhouse gas emissions, by developing ways to reduce greenhouse gas emissions that are applicable to all countries, and by helping emerging and developing countries address environmental issues. Japan recently launched its Cool Earth Promotion Program which seeks to build on the country experience as a leader in energy efficiency and includes a new US$10 billion financial mechanism to help developing countries in their mitigation and adaptation efforts.

The "Cool Earth Promotion Program" reflects my determination as chair of the G8, PM Fukuda told the legislators gathered in Brasilia. I will strive to make progress, in cooperation with the other leaders of the G8, towards a solution to the problem of global warming; a solution the world is eagerly waiting."

But moreover of the climatic change other problems as the waste are creating true difficulty to the world. An example is the situations that happened in one of the most important cities of Italy, Naples, where since the year 1994 the government declared sanitary emergency because of the impossibility of managing waste.

The air has been contaminated with putrid stench and a report of Reuter from January 17, 2008 assure that the "Medical Journal Lancet Oncology" in 2004 considered part of the Campania region, of which Naples is the capital, "the triangle of death" because air, soil and water are polluted by high levels of cancer-causing toxins believed to have come from waste.

Research released in 200 by Italy's National Research Council found that among people living closest to the least-regulated waste-disposal sites -- where trash is dumped in fields or burnt without any controls -- the mortality rate was 12 percent greater than the normal for women and 9 percent greater for men.

Fatal liver cancers were much more common -- up 29 percent for women and 19 percent for men in the most at-risk areas -- and there were huge increases in congenital malformations of the nervous and urinary systems."

The problem of Naples is common in other cities as Rio de Janeiro and Mexico and in other polluted metropolis.

Conclusion: "In the current century, perhaps in our lifetime, the world will face a shocking scarcity of natural resources as a consequence of overexploitation and pollution around the world. This represents a change of the economic paradigm but, more important, an unprecedented and mind-boggling challenge for humanity. We are on the path to the exhaustion of renewable and nonrenewable natural resources, especially water and conventional oil. The paradigm that predominates in the minds of economists is that capital that is the scarce factor of production, but in the 21st century natural resources must be the priority. Achieving production goals will be more difficult for one simple reason: every day the supply of natural resources will be tighter and this represents a new paradigm for the economy, a 180-degree shift in traditional ideas".[16]

In 2007 and on the months of January and February 2008, the prices of the raw materials underwent significant increases. On Friday 29 of February 2008, the price of "Light sweet crude" petroleum in the New York Mercantile Exchange (Nymex) reached U.S. $ 103,07. In March 2008 the Light Sweet crude surpassed 111US$ closing the day in 110.33 US$. That same day the price of gold surpassed US$ 1000 whereas the price of natural gas, coal and platinum also had an important growth and the same happened with the price of food like wheat, milk and cocoa, among other products. The effect of these increases on the production chain is very important and reinforces the worldwide inflationary tendency.

The increase of prices of raw material is due to a combination of elements that have its origin in the real economy and the financial economy. On the real economy, the determining element of the increase of prices is the quote of petroleum. From the last decade of the 20thcentury the worldwide restrictions in oil supply began to become visible. An increased production and consumption linked to reserves that do not increase the sufficient are the basic characteristics.

This process will be accentuated in the next years of the 21st century unless new and abundant oil reserves are found to take care of the growth of the future demand.

The increase of prices of the raw materials reflects what happens in the supply and worldwide demand of these goods. On the financial economy, we found as cause of the increases of prices of the raw materials the fact that the investors of the great Stock markets have begun to understand the weakness of the markets of action and the markets of money and now they prefer to invest in the markets of raw materials.

The investors understand that the true wealth and the benefits in the near future will only be obtained in the markets of raw materials, which are beginning to be scarce goods. This explains the weakening of the markets of action and bonds and the fortification undergone by the market of raw materials in 2007 and in the first months of 2008. This tendency must be getting stronger in short to medium term.

The weakening of the dollar towards the Euro and other currencies has contributed to strengthen the market of raw materials. For those who have Euros, the raw materials have lowered the price in 50 percent approximately due to the devaluation of the dollar. On Thursday 28 of February 2008, the dollar overcame for the first time the barrier of 1.50 US$ per Euro and on Friday 29 of February 2008 it reached US. $ 1.52 Per Euro; this fact contributed to increase the demand of raw materials, since the majority of them quote in dollars.

If the demand increases, the price is fortified and it may even increase if the supply is not sufficient as it happened in 2007 and January and February of 2008.

Dollar is the universal currency in which more than 85 percent of the daily currency transactions in the world are made; in addition, almost two thirds of the currency reserves of the central banks of the world are denominated in dollars. The dollar is then the currency in which most worldwide commerce is made. This fact turns it into an instrument very difficult to replace.

The reduction of the interest rates in the United States, the real estate crisis of 2007 and beginnings of the 2008 and the threats of recession are economical questions that the United States would have to surpass in a short term in spite of the actions developed by some countries to make the dollar weaker in the international markets. Iraq, for example, on February 17, 2008 inaugurated its Oil Stock market in the Island of Kish in the Persian Gulf. The Stock-market had as primary target –in its first stage-- to sell petroleum, petrochemical products and other Iranian products in the national currency of the country and, then, secondly, to quote these products in Euros and rubles. Until February 17 2008, the dollar was the currency of transactions in the Iranian market, but from that date Iran has his own marker of prices.

The Council of Cooperation of the Arab States of the Gulf (CCSAG) expressed interest in the decision made by Iran and assured that already Kuwait separated of the fixed parity with the dollar, decision that would be imitated by Qatar and the United Arab Emirates. The experts consider that only Saudi Arabia remains loyal to the dollar like currency for the accomplishment of its international operations of petroleum sale.

Russia has also announced that it will create a market of commodities in which the future petroleum contracts and other products will be quoted in rubles.

It is doubtless that these actions create a difficult situation to the North American currency but those situations are not sufficient to anticipate a substitution of the dollar as the most accepted currency of the world.

Everything will depend then on the success and the acceptance that the new currencies acquire in the international trade but the dollar will not be dethroned as the most important international currency.

The greatest problem for the worldwide economy is the threat of the crisis of the raw materials due to the increase of the demand and to the limitations of supply.

The most serious fact that the worldwide economy must confront in a middle term is the water shortage that already begins to be visible in different parts of the world and, especially, in the Middle East and Asia; this will bring a true worldwide revolution.

The problem of the supplying of raw materials will then be the main concern of the world in the years to come. Everything indicates that the world is on the way of a global crisis of natural resources, especially water and petroleum, due to overexploitation of the resources and to contamination.

The unique way to save the planet

The only way to preserve the planet is to stop the destruction of forests, the drastic decrease of the emission of greenhouse gases into the atmosphere, prevent contamination of water sources and development of a global program of reforestation. If such actions do not begin to be implemented soon, most the planet is in danger of becoming a desert. One of the key measures is to preserve the Amazon, which is seriously threatened, and where every day is destroyed hundreds of hectares of forests.

Chapter 4

Keeping peace a difficult task

Humanity seems to be condemned to war. The history of the ancient and modern world has countless examples of this fact. The history of the present times ---the 20th century and the 21st century--- also confirms it. In the first decade of the 20th century the 1st World war took place (1914-1918); twenty years later the world entered in a conflict again, the 2nd World War (1938-1945).

When the 2nd World war ended many people thought a new stage of peace could begin. But these hopes disappeared very soon. The Soviets and the western countries worked together to defeat the Nazi forces. But when the conflict concluded in 1945 the Soviets quickly showed their disposition to dominate the world and to keep the territories that had been released. Berlin was the first great objective of the Russians.

After a long process for the dominion of the city, on March 1948, the Soviets decided to block the accesses to Berlin, creating a difficult situation that once again placed the world peace in danger. As a result of the actions of the Soviets, the only way available to supply Berlin was by air. The United States and the allies did not have any other option but to accept the blockade to avoid the confrontation.

On June 1949 the Russians suspended the blockade of the city. The most important consequence of these facts was the creation of two states in Germany and the definitive rupture between the Soviets and the western countries. All these events began a new process of confrontation known as the Cold War.

The same happened in those years in Korea and Vietnam, countries that were in the power of Japan and were released by the Red Army. In these two countries the Communists settled down governments dependent of Moscow and fomented the division of those countries in two states, North Korea, of communist inspiration and South Korea, pro western and North Vietnam, pro communist and South Vietnam, pro western.

In the countries of Eastern Europe Russians also established satellite governments of Moscow and created the so-called Iron Curtain.

In the Post War, the Soviet communist government created and fortified its nuclear power and initiated a new confrontation against their old Western allies in diverse scenes.

From then on, the ghost of war again appeared in the political worldwide scene but this time in a completely different way from the well known before. The new military form was the nuclear war, whose first sample was first known by the world in Hiroshima and Nagasaki (1945).

As a result of the new confrontation between the great powers, the United States and the Soviet Union, there was a fear that any political crisis situation or even any human error by a wrong strategic military processing of information could unleash the nuclear war.

During the years of the Cold War the discordant note always was China, country that held a radical position and criticized the efforts of the Soviet Union in the days of Prime Minister Nikita Khrushchev, in favor of the well-known policy with the name of Pacific Coexistence. The Chinese leader, Mao Tse Tung, in that time described the United States as being like a paper tiger coming to the point that by the end of the fifties and beginnings of the sixties, they practically broke their relations with the Soviet Union, accusing this country to betray the orthodox communist ideas represented by the conceptions of Marx and Lenin.

But the appreciation of Mao Tse Tung on the supposed weakness of the Soviet Union in front of the United States was mistaken. Indeed, the Soviet Union during the years of the Cold War gave demonstrations of radical attitudes that placed the world on the brink of confrontation. The most representative example of this is, perhaps, the crisis of the rockets of 1962 generated as a result of the installation of atomic weapons in a base in Cuba.

On October 1962 an American spy airplane, U2, discovered that the

Soviets were installing a series of long-range missiles in Cuba. After days of great tension, the president of the United States, John Kennedy, orders to his Armed Forces a naval blockade against Cuba to prevent the passage of the Soviet ships that took the rest of the missiles to complete the installation of the Russian arms in the Island. Since that moment the world entered the most difficult stage of history, because a nuclear war meant, obviously, the end of humanity. The uncertainty of which would be the reaction of the Soviet leaders and if they would accept or not the blockade against its forces was present during several days. But at the end, the Soviet leadership, headed by Prime Minister Nikita Khrushchev, avoided the confrontation and ordered its naval forces to return to its bases, and so the most intense crisis of the Cold War concluded.

Other episodes of confrontation took place between 1962 and 1991, year in which an unthinkable fact until that moment happens: the dissolution of the Soviet Union, in the middle of a great political and economic crisis.

As a result of the Berlin Wall fall (1989) and the dissolution of the Soviet Union (1991), the possibility of a lasting peace was opened again and many thought that the danger of a nuclear war had disappeared. But long time had not passed when a new threat arose in the worldwide scene.

This time it was the Persian Gulf War, as a result of the invasion on Kuwait by Iraq on August 2, 1990. Six months later, on January 16 of 1991, acting on behalf of a resolution of the United Nations, the United States in charge of a multinational force initiated the rescue of Kuwait through the Operation called: Desert Storm and in one month - - on February of 1991 – they drove out the Iraqi forces in a war that left a balance of a great number of victims and uncountable damages to the reserves of petroleum and gas of Kuwait.

Although during this conflict nuclear weapons were not used, the Iraqi forces used another type of massive destruction arms, the chemical arms that remembered the world what could mean nowadays a conflict of such a great magnitude. This was the last war of the 20th century, although other conflicted scenes (civil wars) were also developed in different countries during the last decade of the 20th century.

With the disappearance of the USSR and the Cold War certainly the danger of a great confrontation between the two great nuclear powers was reduced significantly but new dangers arose that threaten the world peace and that can also lead us to the nuclear disaster.

Those dangers have become especially visible in the first years of the 21st century as a result of the dominion of the atomic energy with military aims of countries as North Korea, Iran, Pakistan, India and Israel.

A step to World War III

In order to confirm the rule of history, the 21st Century began with a new confrontation, this time in Afghanistan, as an answer of the United States to the destruction of the Twin Towers in New York on September 11 of 2002. The government of the United States accused the Taliban government of Afghanistan to protect the leaders of the terrorist organization Al Qaeda, which make the attacks in Washington and in New York in 2002 and, as a consequence, invaded Afghanistan and overthrew the Taliban government.

The following year, on March 20 of 2003, another confrontation of great magnitude affected the world: the second Gulf War through the invasion of Iraq by United States.

Year 2004 was also time of great tensions due to the continuity of the confrontation between North Korea and the United States.

On 2005 the managements to solve the crisis continued by means of the call of meetings to six parts: The United States, Russia, China, Japan, North Korea and South Korea. It was a process of advances and backward movements since North Korea objected the first accomplishment of the conversations between the six parts and requested to negotiate directly with the United States, country that rejected the request and insisted on that it was a problem of the six countries.

After multiple managements, North Korea, on September of 2005, accepted to adhere to the Treaty of non-proliferation of Nuclear weapons, but only 24 hours after signing the treaty, it rejected the document and returned to its starting point, that is to say, to ask for the construction of a heavy water plant like condition to suspend his military nuclear activities.

The negotiations remained suspended due to this circumstance, which put in evidence that North Korea only was only looking for some more time to continue its program of nuclear weapons.

Sometime later, on October 8 2006, the government of North Korea officially informed that a first nuclear test had been successfully achieved by this country; information that was confirmed later by sources of the United States and South Korea.

The test took place in the North Korean population of Hwadaeri and brought about tremors of a magnitude of 3,58 degrees in the scale of Ritcher, according to the sources. The nuclear test fortified the negotiating position of Pyongyang and multiplied the preoccupation of the rest of the countries, especially of its neighbors.

In the background the confrontation with North Korea and Iran has been a fight for the natural resources, water, food, oil and atomic energy. In the conversations about the nuclear program of North Korea initiated on February Thursday 8th of 2007 in Peking, the delegate of North Korea, Kim Kye Gwan, confirmed this appreciation and said that his country is willing "to discuss the initial steps towards the disarmament" in exchange to energetic help and the normalization of the relations with Washington.

The fundamental objective of North Korea was to obtain oil and food because since the year 1994 its population suffered severe crisis due to the lack of these resources. On February 13th of 2007, North Korea announced an agreement with United States, Russia, Japan, China and South Korea to dismount its nuclear facilities in exchange for energetic help for which North Korea would receive urgently 50,000 tons of oil, during the following 60 days beginning with the firm of the agreement and 950,000 tons more when deactivating the nuclear power station in Yongbion and the rest of the programs.

In the year 2005 the danger of an atomic war acquired a new

impulse, this time due to the confrontation between Iran, United States and the countries of the European Union.

The conflict between the western countries and Iran got worse in 2005 due to the refusal of this country to suspend its activities of uranium enrichment. The Iranian authorities sustained that they were in their right to use the atomic energy to generate electricity but the neighbors of Iran and the western countries thought that the true objective of Iran was to elaborate an important amount of nuclear weapons. On September 20 of 2005, Alí Larijani, head of the Iranian nuclear program, officially announced that the country could leave the Treaty of Nuclear Non-proliferation if they keep on using against them the language of force.

On March 21 of 2007, the top Iranian leader, Ayatola Alí Jomenei, warned that Iran will continue its nuclear activities outside the international norms if the Security Council of the United Nations insists on the cease of the uranium enrichment in Iran; and pointed out to the United States that "Iran will use all means to attack the enemies who attack Iran."

The decision of Iran to continue its nuclear program will be a key factor for the development of the crisis. Iran has managed to construct to an important structure for the energy atomic generation with the aid of the Soviet Union since the eighties. Important Russian spokesmen reiterated that cooperation would continue being increased. But Iran not only receives the cooperation of Russia but also of China and Pakistan. So one thing declares the Russian spokesmen and the Chinese spokesmen and another thing is what they do in the reality in respect to nuclear matters.

Iran assures that it will develop its program only with pacific aims: for the electricity generation, but none of its neighbors, nor the United States nor the countries of the European Union believe in the Iranian speech.

These countries suspect that Iran will use its atomic development for the production of arms of massive destruction. The problem is much more serious than it seems, because neighbors of Iran own nuclear weapons and they have declared this openly. This is the case of Pakistan and India. The logical question that arises then is why the United States and Europe have allowed Pakistan and India their nuclear development with military aims and why is Iran not allowed to do it. Why India and Pakistan yes, and why Iran not?

The answer is not logical; it is simply an illogical political answer. The policy not always is logical. It is a problem of the political objectives of the countries, the coincidence or the contrast of political objectives. In this case the contrast of objectives between Iran, the United States and the rest of the western world.

The answer to the question was synthesized in a clear and simple form by General Michael Hayden, assistant director of The National Intelligence of the United States on February 8 of 2006; Hayden said, "A nuclear Iran is absolutely unacceptable."

The origin of this radical position of the United States and the main countries of Europe could be found in the attitude assumed by Iran since the overthrow of Shah Reza Phalevi, in 1979. Since that moment a theocratic, radical government took the power in that country that considered as a central objective to confront the western culture.

Leading the government was a monk of extremist conceptions, the Ayatolah Jomeini, who on April 1 of 1979 wins a referendum and from that moment on he eliminates all the vestiges of the Shah´s regime and restores an Islamic republic. On November 4, 1979, hardly a few months after the Ayatolah Jomeini had the power some Islamic radical groups assaulted the embassy of the United States in the capital of Iran and took as hostages the diplomatic personnel, 52 North American citizens.

The invasion of the embassy and the situation of the hostages extended for more than a year, until January 20 of 1981, provoking since then a permanent confrontation with United States.

The conflict for the energy

So far, the cause of the confrontation between the United States and North Korea and the United States and the European Union against Iran is precisely because of the use of the atomic energy. That is what appears in foreground, what is evident; the United States and the European Union fears that North Korea and Iran use their atomic power for provoking a nuclear war.

The balance of power in Asia and the Middle East was altered as a result of the conversion of India and Pakistan as nuclear powers, but in spite of it the peace has remained in the region. The new problem is that the incorporation of new members to the nuclear club in Asia, as North Korea and Iran could change not only the situation of Asia and the Middle East, but also the situation in Europe and America, that is to say, could bring about a new situation of worldwide conflict.

Ready for anything

The terrorist attacks of September 11, 2002 in New York, in Madrid (2001), in London (2005) and Egypt (2005), unveil the great threat that is present in the world. Indeed, those attacks reveal that there are extremist sectors ready for anything. If the terrorists continue their actions, the answer of the attacked ones will be immediate and this will place the world on the edge of a new war that can be a world war.

The fuel that feeds war is hatred, which has not diminished among the countries that are fanatic of religion or politics.

In the Middle East and Asia are the countries that in the last years have reached the higher levels of religious and political fanaticism.

From the Middle East and Asia have arisen the main terrorist actions that have affected the world at the beginning of the 21st century and everything indicates that it will be in this region where worldwide peace will be defined in a medium to long term.

War probabilities

On February of 2006, the results of some studies of opinion were spread in the United States according to which 2/3 of the North Americans consider that Iran would attack the United States and Europe if it develops nuclear weapons and a percentage superior thinks that when Iran ends its atomic program it will provide nuclear weapons worldwide to the terrorist groups. The consequence of this is logical: almost 60% of the North Americans would indorse an armed intervention in Iran if this country develops atomic arms.

Second Part
The History

Introduction

In this part of the essay it is proven how the struggle for the natural resources has already generated the first threat of usage of the nuclear power of one country against another one. This means that the world peace is going to depend directly on what happens with the natural resources. A topic of great current importance which essence will not loose force, since the depletion of the natural resources for overexploitation and for pollution is a reality that the world will continue confronting for a long period of time. It is a vision of short as well as long term, an analysis that raises different hypotheses about the future of the world peace.

Will the fight for natural resources be the main cause of the world conflicts in the 21st century? Does North Korea really have atomic weapons? Is it willing to use them? What is hidden behind North Korea? Does North Korea act in completely independent form? Does North Korea serve to a strategy of distraction of China to continue consolidating its military power? Will the eastern countries dominate the western countries in the future? Is Japan today an ally of the Western World; will it be an ally of the western forever? Until what point will the cultural identity influence so that the eastern countries unite to face the western countries? Which will be the paper of the Islamic countries as Iran that is also developing a considerable nuclear power? ¿Which will be the role of Israel that is developing one important nuclear power too? Does Russia no longer represent a nuclear threat? Those are some of the big queries that are presented in this part of the essay and those that we will try to give an answer.

Chapter 5

The Gulf War

In February of the year 2003 United States and Great Britain invaded Iraq. To justify the invasion to their populations and to the world, the governments of the two countries argued that the dictator of that country, Saddam Hussein, was accumulating a very important quantity of weapons of massive destruction that would eventually use against their neighbors and the rest of the world. This was perfectly believable since Hussein was an implacable tyrant that had made numerous crimes. One of the remembered episodes that won him the rejection of the world was the murder with chemical weapons in March of 1988 of thousands of Kurdish citizens' - including women and children- in the village of Halabaja to the north of Iran. Hussein had an arsenal of chemical and biological weapons and had also used it in his long war against his neighbor Iran and, later, in the so called Gulf War against his other neighbor, Kuwait in 1990.

In the year 2003 and facing the new information that Hussein had increased his arsenal of these types of weapons and that he was willing to use them again, United States and Great Britain invaded Iraq against the opinion of the other three members of the United Nations Security Council, France, Russia and China.

The troops entered in Iraq but they could not show to the world the places where supposedly the new weapons of massive destruction were being manufactured. This left an unpleasant flavor in some international sectors which began to think that United States and Great Britain had exaggerated their appreciation deliberately on the weapons of massive destruction of Iraq and that the true purpose when invading this country was to appropriate their important reserves of petroleum, second of the world. By the year 2000 Iraq had 112,500 million barrels in its reserves, which represented 10.44 percent of the world reserves.[17]

Few months after the invasion and the presence of United States and Great Britain in Iraq, in Great Britain occurred an event that would come to justify the doubts of those who had expressed their reserves over the true purposes of the invasion. Indeed, on July 2003 an advisory of the Defense ministry of Great Britain and expert scientist in weapons, David Kelly, appeared dead. He would have revealed to the BBC of London that the U.K. government exaggerated deliberately on the existence of weapons of massive destruction in Iraq. This caused a political storm in Great Britain that threatened the own first minister Tony Blair, who lost the support of almost 60 percent of the population of that country for this cause, according to the published opinion studies.

But the Kelly scandal didn't only have repercussions in Great Britain but rather motivates to think if it cannot be happening the same thing with relationship to the information's diffused in the year 2003 about North Korea and Iran, countries that would be also in a nuclear career of importance. Will it be happening to North Korea the same thing that happened to Iraq? Will the government from United States be exaggerating on the presence in Iran of nuclear weapons? These were logical questions that arose after the Kelly scandal. The appearance of things is generally different to its essence. Essence and appearance are not usually the same.

The international information's of the year 2003 revealed that North Korea had challenged the power of United States. The relationship of conventional military force existent between United States and North Korea is as the force relationship existent between a sardine and a shark, but when one speaks of the presence of atomic weapons the situation changes completely. In this case there are not big neither small countries, because the atomic weapons equal forces between countries that have it. That is the great problem.

Observation

The countries that threaten the world peace have something in common: one or several necessities that they cannot solve with their proper resources.

Hypothesis

As consequence of the production and consumption pattern followed up to now, which is characterized by the overexploitation of the natural resources and the growing contamination, the world is arriving to a point of shortage of natural resources that will increase the economic, political and social contradictions inside the countries and in the international relationships.

As most of the countries are poor and have big frustrations, the possibilities of an escalation of the conflicts are bigger. In the measure in which the natural resources get scarcer the competition for them will increase and its price will be increased generating to the poorer nations bigger difficulties to buy them.

But like part of the poor countries have learned how to use the atom with military purposes and as surely the number of countries with that knowledge and capacity will be enlarged in the future, the possibilities of nuclear conflicts among countries or among regions or even of a great nuclear conflict are scenarios that cannot be discarded when considering the perspectives of the world peace in the 21st century.

What North Korea and Iraq had in common in Saddam Hussein's time?

The answer is very simple. They had in common hunger, thirst and governments willing to dominate the nuclear energy at any cost.

Iran possesses petroleum in abundance but don't have enough water nor food. North Korea doesn't have petroleum neither water nor food.

When one observes the rest of the countries with serious armed internal conflicts it can also be proven in most of the cases like a common fact to all of them the lack of food, water or petroleum or the lack of all them together. And in the cases where the resources exist, like in Colombia, the problem is that those resources are not well distributed creating the conditions for violence. According to the reports of United Nations, by the year 2003 in the Middle East five countries confronted serious armed conflicts; in Asia eight countries; in Europe the conflict between Russia and Chechnya and in Latin America the armed conflict of Colombia.

Chapter 6

What is the cause of conflicts?

A single answer doesn't exist. The causes are many and diverse. But, historically, in an important number of cases it has been always especially for economic reasons. The wars were generally wars of occupation. A country invaded another and the fundamental purpose of the invasion was to appropriate the resources of that country, water, food, energy, gold or other wealth.

It could be said that the fight for natural resources has been an important cause of the conflicts. In many cases have been invoked political, racial and religious reasons, but in the undertone the fight for the resources has been the true deep motivation of all those conflicts. This has been a historical constant. The lack of natural resources is cause but also effect of the conflicts.

Petroleum, water and food as cause of the future world conflicts

Up to now, second decade of the 21st century, the world has not faced a *global shortage* of natural resources. In some countries specifically and in some regions of the world there have been and are problems of energy shortage, water and food. But in the measure that the global contamination increases and that the overexploitation of the resources also increases, the problem of shortage will be no longer a fact restricted to some countries and regions of the world to become a *global problem.*

The signs of the exhaustion of natural resources to world scale every day are bigger.[18] The reserves of conventional oil have remained stagnated for a long period of time, tendency that became more visible in the 21st century. Countries that in the past had a great amount of reserves as United States have drained the conventional petroleum that remains in their ground. Areas like the North Sea that from the seventies began to give an important production are already in clear drop. Russia had an increase of its reserves 2000-2005 but not enough important as to modify the world tendency to the stagnation of the reserves; the same happens in the Middle East. But the consumption increases in constant form. So that if this tendency is maintained to a medium term the world could face a situation of chronic lack of conventional petroleum that would alter the economic and political relationships completely.

But it is not only petroleum. It is also other vital resources as the water that is finishing already in many regions of the world, especially in Asia, continent that harbors most of the world's population.[19] The lack of water in China is of such magnitude that it is considered will make crisis very soon and as consequence of it China will have to import most of its cereals. This will generate chaos in the prices of these commodities, affecting the poorest countries that won't be able to pay the new prices; this will generate a new pressure on the world peace. The same happens in India that must dedicate a very important part of its energy to pump water of the underground. It also happens in Pakistan, in Afghanistan, in Vietnam, that is to say in almost all Asia and also in a good part of Africa. So that we have approximately 73 percent of the world's population seriously threatened by lack of water and food.[20]

As consequence of the water problem and of the global contamination, signs of deterioration are perceived in the food production. For example, the cereal production registered a descent worthy of being mentioned. Indeed, according to the reports of the United Nations Feeding and Agriculture Organization, FAO, the global production of cereals showed stagnation signs among the year 1999, when it was located in 236,835,608 metric tons, the year 2000 when it diminished to 235,493,500 metric tons and the year 2001 when it lowers to be located in 230,611,000 metric tons again. The climatic change caused in turn by the deterioration of the ozone layer as a consequence of the intense use of the fossil fuels and other polluting elements has had direct influence on these results. This phenomenon was being observed for some time and was accentuated in the decade of the nineties.

The world production of wheat had increases and significant descents in the decade of the nineties and the years 2000. In 1997, for example, it was of 69,350,200 metric tons but in 1998 it descended to 66,345,000 million metric tons to later ascend to 75,574,000 metric tons in the year 2000 and to go down to 68,458,000 million metric tons in the year 2001.

The world production of rice, corn, barley and sorghum has also experienced similar sways being observed a tendency to the stagnation of production between 1999 and the year 2001.

The cereals provide 50 percent of the total of available calories for the human consumption. A third of the cereals production is dedicated to the production of foods for animals that are in turn the source of proteins for the population; therefore, any alteration that takes place in its production affects the food and agricultural chain directly.

The price of food

A shortage of foods will be reflected directly on its prices. The shortage of vital goods as water, food and conventional petroleum will change the political, economic and social structure of the world in the 21st century. As a consequence of that shortage, the prices of all the goods and services that the human being produce and consume will radically be altered. This, obviously, will benefit only a few ones and will harm the great majority. The petroleum producers, for example, would be immediate beneficiaries of an ascent of the prices, but very soon they would become victims when having to pay other commodities and the manufactured products that they import from other nations. Countries that produce most of the world's cereals, as United States, the European Union, Canada, Australia and Argentina would benefit in a first moment of an increment of the grains price, but very soon they would also receive the negative impact that for them will mean a reduction of the sales as a consequence of the prices increase, because most of the countries won't be able to pay the new prices.

The shortage of commodities outlines a new world reality; a scenario unknown up to now and whose consequences are difficult to foresee. This forecast shall occur because of a simple reason: the untenable population growth rate.

Map of the drought in Asia

The Alert number 308 of the FAO of May 11, 2000 was sufficiently revealing of what happens in Asia; this situation every day is worse.

The Alert highlights that millions of people were seriously affected by the drought in several countries, as a consequence of the climatic changes that have desolated cultivations and livestock and in addition the loss of human lives as a consequence in turn of the shortage of water and food.

Afghanistan

This country did not only live a precarious situation of food supply due to the problem of the civil war but to the drought that affected the south and the east especially the regions of Kandahar, Helmand and Zabul. Thousands of people that lost their possessions in the fields have emigrated towards the cities in search of food.

By the year 1999 the total production of Afghanistan's cereals decreased in 3.24 million tons, 16 percent below the numbers of the previous year due to the drought and to the lack of pesticides. This motivated the necessity to increase the imports of cereals in 1.1 million tons. The Report of FAO highlights that if the drought continues it will be necessary to increase the imports and to grant to that country food help.

Iran

A similar situation confronted Iran in the year 2000. The wheat production fell in 3 million tons, 25 percent less in relationship to the previous year and the Report of FAO points out that 18 of the 28 counties of Iran were affected by the shortage of food due to the drought.

The impact of the drought was increased in 2000 due to the low levels of the dams and water reservoirs. In 1998, Iran reached its biggest production of cereals -18,979,267 metric tons- of the twelve years between 1990 and the 2002. The production registered variations and in the last year it was located in 17,323,000 metric tons, which puts in evidence that the logical increment that should register according to the population's increase did not take place.

Wheat production reached 12,000,000 metric tons in 2002, being this quantity insufficient to assist the population's necessities. Corn had also a tendency to increment to be located in 1,200,000 metric tons in 2002, but also insufficient to assist the requirements of feeding of that country. Other cultivations like the rice presented a falling tendency since it passing from 2,770,554 metric tons in 1998 - maximum production- to 2,115,000 metric tons in 2002. The perspectives of production were negative in commodities as barley, product of great importance for feeding the livestock, of which depends in turn good part the population's food. This generated panic among the farmers that began to sell their livestock and to leave their lands.

Between the years 1999 and 2000 Iran was one of the biggest world importers of wheat, reaching 7 million tons; this puts in evidence the vulnerability of this country in alimentary matters.

Iraq

The reports of FAO also reveals that Iraq suffered a similar situation in 2000 and that the Tigris and Euphrates rivers diminished its flow in more than 20 percent, affecting the production by 70 percent of the cultivated areas. In 1999 similar conditions reduced the production of cereals of Iraq in near 40 percent in comparison to the five year-old average. A similar impact took place on the livestock production, generating a situation of alimentary crisis.

In 1999 Iraq reached its biggest production of cereals -3,400,000 tons metric- quantity that diminished notably in 2002 when it reached the quantity of 1,400,000 metric tons, less than half of the maximum reached in the twelve years between 1990 and 2002.

Wheat production that reached a maximum volume of 1,400,000 metric tons in 1991 diminished to 800,000 metric tons in 2002, almost half.

Production of rice also diminished of the maximum reached in 1994 from 383,000 metric tons to only 90,000 metric tons in 2002. The same happened with barley that passed from 1,800,000 metric tons in 1990 to only 500,000 metric tons in 2002. And the production of corn that descended from its maximum 280,000 metric tons in 1993 to 60,000 tons in 2002, while the figures of sorghum production decreased to less than the half passing from 1,600,000 metric tons in 1990 to 700,000 metric tons in 2002. In the decade of the nineties Iraq suffered an international seizure as sanction for their invasion to

Kuwait in 1990. These figures reflect the consequences of that seizure, since that country depended on the imports of inputs like fertilizers and machineries to impel its agriculture. But the most outstanding fact that should influence in these results is the effect of the climatic change that caused serious problems of drought in Iraq, breaking the possibilities of expansion of production.

Jordan

Another country of the region with similar problems is Jordan whose agricultural production suffered the effects of the climatic change and, in particular, of the lingering droughts. The wheat crops and barley had been specially affected and their production on the whole decreased by 88 percent in 1999. The livestock was also seriously affected as well as the horticultural cultivations and therefore FAO gave financial attendance to assist the affected farmers.

Pakistan

Pakistan is another of the countries of the region with severe problems of drought. Its eastern and southern counties have been seriously committed for some time and there are regions where it hasn't rain for several years. As a consequence the supply of water and foods has become a serious problem. Reports of FAO indicate that the livestock flock has diminished and also that hundreds of people have died as a consequence of this whole situation.

India

The other giant from Asia with problems of food supply due to the lack of water is India. By the year 2001, India reached its maxim figure of cereals production of the last twelve years, 243,375,204 metric tons. And by 2002 it had a significant descent to be located in 213,590,104 metric tons.

The wheat production passed from 76,368,896 metric tons in 2000 to 71,814,304 metric tons in 2002. The production of rice passed from 134,496,304 metric tons in 1999 to 116,580,000 metric tons in 2002. The production of barley passed from 1,485,700 metric tons in 1990 to 1,415,800 in 2002. The corn passed from 13,301,900 metric tons in 2001 to 10,570,000 in 2002 and the sorghum from 12,806,000 in 1992 to 7,060,000 in 2002. These figures do not need any additional comment.

China

China, the other giant from the Asia is not the exception and comes suffering the effects of serious periods of drought that have affected his crops and maintains dry many of its most important rivers during long periods of time and in diverse areas of their way. As a consequence of all this, China diminished its agricultural production, especially of cereals.

The total production of cereals of China reached its maximum point -of the twelve years between 1990 and 2002- in 1998 when it reached the quantity of 458,395,558 metric tons but in 2002 it registered a descent to be located in 402,000,611 metric tons.

The China's production of wheat also presented in the signal period a significant descent passing from its maximum point 123,290,085 metric tons in 1997 to 91,290,240 metric tons in 2002. Something similar happened with rice that passed from 202,771,843 metric tons in 1997 to 176,553,000 metric tons in 2002. The same happened to barley that descends from 4,500,000 metric tons in 1994 to 2,470,000 in 2002; with corn that passed from 133,197,000 metric tons in 1998 to 123,175,000 metric tons in 2002 and with sorghum that passed of 6,438,308 in 1994 at 2,731,000 in 2002.

These figures show a tendency in the continent with more population in the world. The trend is to the exhaustion of the natural resources, especially water and food. This has a great political and economic significance and, in consequence, for the world peace because Asia is the continent with the biggest number of countries that are learning the use of the nuclear weapons. Indeed, countries like India, Pakistan, Iran and North Korea have been able to develop a capacity of nuclear offensive in the last decade of the 20th century and in the first years of the 21st century and in addition, China consolidated its nuclear power long time ago. These are countries with serious problems of poverty in most of their population, with problems of hunger, lack of water and in some cases as North Korea, of a very important lack of petroleum. And those countries will go to look for the water, food and the petroleum that they need in the neighbors countries or in any other part of the world in peaceful or violent form.

Many countries confront problems of alimentary emergency

The hunger in the world is not something new. It has always existed. Some countries have had the privilege of having wealth and others not. Up to now those who have suffered hunger have been mainly the poorest, the less prepared scientific and technologically and those that are located in areas prone to natural disasters. But this situation is beginning to change and now the richest countries also have to confront situations of vulnerability of an every time bigger number of people. In the measure in that the fight for the natural resources is accentuated, in that same measure it will be more intense the internal fight inside the own richer countries for wealth, water, food, for products of petroleum like gasoline, oils, fuels for heating and for the other natural resources. And what happens today at international level will happen inside the territories of each one of the developed countries.

In the table that follows can be appreciated the number of countries that confronted problems of alimentary emergency the year 2001. The cause in most cases was the climatic problems; in some cases intense droughts and in other lingering winters, shortage of water, lack of inputs and the armed violence.

FAO/GIEWS - Foodcrops & Shortages No.3, June 2001 - Page 2
AFFECTED COUNTRIES
COUNTRIES FACING EXCEPTIONAL FOOD EMERGENCIES
(Total: 33 countries)
Country/Region
Reason for Emergency

AFRICA (17 countries)
Angola * Civil strife, population displacement
Burkina Faso Drought
Burundi * Civil strife and insecurity
Chad Drought
Congo, Dem. Rep. * Civil strife, IDPs and refugees
Eritrea * IDPs, returnees and drought

Ethiopia*2 / Drought, IDPs
Guinea Civil strife, population displacement
Kenya Drought
Liberia * Past civil strife, shortage of inputs
Niger Drought
Rwanda * Drought in parts
Sierra Leone * Civil strife, population displacement
Somalia * Drought, civil strife
They sweat * Civil strife in the south, drought
Tanzania Food deficits in several regions
Uganda Civil strife in parts, drought

ASIA (12 countries)
Afghanistan * Drought, civil strife
Armenia * Drought, economic constraints
Azerbaijan Drought, economic constraints
Cambodia Past floods
Georgia * Drought, economic constraints
Iraq * Sanctions, drought
Jordan Drought
Korea, DPR * Adverse weather, economic problems
Mongolia * Harsh winter, economic problems
Tajikistan * Water shortages, drought
Turkmenistan Drought and water shortages
Uzbekistan Drought and water shortages

LATIN AMERICA (2 countries)
Haiti * Structural economic problems, vulnerable groups
El Salvador Earthquakes
EUROPE (2 countries)
Russian Federation (Chechnya) Civil strife, vulnerable groups
F.Rep. Yugoslavia * (Serbia & Montenegro) Vulnerable groups and refugees

COUNTRIES WITH UNFAVOURABLE PROSPECTS FOR CURRENT CROPS
Country
Harvest dates Main contributory factors
Afghanistan * May/June Adverse weather, civil strife

China (mainland) May/June Drought in the north
Iran, Islamic Rep. of June. / Aug. Drought
Iraq * May/June Erratic rainfall, shortage of inputs
Jordan May/June Drought
Korea DPR * June/July Drought
Somalia * Aug. / Sept. Civil strife, low rainfall
They sweat * Nov. / Dec. Civil strife, low rainfall
Syria May/July Low rainfall
Tajikistan * Jun. / Aug. Drought, shortage of seed, economic constraints
Turkmenistan June/July Drought, input shortages
Uzbekistan June/Aug. Drought, water shortages
F.Rep. Yugoslavia *
(Serbia & Montenegro) July/Oct. Drought and shortage of inputs

----

1 / Both here and in the text, countries with unfavorable prospects for current crop and/or uncovered shortfalls plows marked in bold and those affected or threatened by successive poor crops or food shortages it plows marked with an asterisk (*). Definitions dog be found on the Contents page.
2 / Country requiring external assistance for purchase and distribution of localized surpluses to deficit areas.

The confrontation between countries always has a cause

The countries don't go to war for anything. It is not truth that man like specie has a warrior instinct that has always maintained humanity in conflict. Only a minority has that instinct and when that minority arrives to the power then the wars take place. Regrettably in all the nations and in all the times there have existed those minorities that also have the ability to appropriate the power in any way. That is what explains that in all the times in some part of the world or in several regions violent conflicts have taken place at the same time. History shows that a specific type of leaders, radical people that exercise the power in a certain moment, unchains the wars. The aggressors that cause wars are generally personalities different regarding the common people, people with big frustrations, with messianic ambitions.

Chapter 7

North Korea threatens with the nuclear war

Up to now and from the ending of the Second World War - Hiroshima and Nagasaki- the armed conflicts have been limited to the use of conventional weapons. But in the year 2002 for first time a country threatened another with the use of its nuclear force. It was the threat that North Korea formulated on December 2002, through its Secretary of External Relationships, Kim Il Ch'ol, who declared that his country had something more powerful than a simple atomic bomb and it should prepare to respond to the aggression of United States. In June 2003 the official agency of North Korea disclosed an information in which affirmed that "if the US keeps threatening the Popular Democratic Republic of Korea with nukes instead of abandoning its hostile policy towards Pyongyang, the DPRK will have not option but to build up a nuclear deterrent force." On September 9, 2003 during the commemoration of the 55 anniversary of the country foundation, the Popular Army chief, Kim Young Chun, accused the United States of continuing its hostility policy towards Pyongyang and ratified the Korean decision of enhance its nuclear force deterrent to the country defense.

North Korea had expressed fear for a possible invasion of troops of

United States and argued that its nuclear arsenal had as first objective to act as dissuasive factor in front of that threat. In South Korea remained 37,000 North American soldiers. North Korea had expressed its disposition of reducing its military force in soldiers' number -the fifth in the world- if United States moves away its forces of South Korea.

Pyongyang interpreted the declaration formulated in January 2002 by the United States President, George Bush, as a direct aggression. In that occasion the President of United States said that North Korea, Iran and Iraq formed the devil's triangle that threatens humanity with weapons of massive destruction. Starting from that moment the relations between United States and North Korea began to be more tenser until that in October 2002 the North Korea authorities recognized that they were manufacturing nuclear weapons, in violation to the Agreement signed with United States in Geneva in 1994, by means of which that country was committed to suspend and to disable its atomic weapons program.

But North Korea not stopped in its threats and maintained an open challenge. In April of the year 2003, for example, in the conversations carried out in Beijing with United States and China on the nuclear situation, North Korea expressed that would consider any sanction that imposes them the United Nations as an act of war and would act in consequence.

Joseph Stalin, (1859-1953) the dictator of the Soviet Union who had the control of the nuclear power of that country for several years until his death in the fifties, had great care of not using that great power although he was who began the Cold War. Not even Stalin - considered a man without limits- was able to use or to threat other countries with his nuclear power. Its successor, Nikita Khrushchev, (1894-1971) did not do it either. Khrushchev took out his shoe in an occasion in the United Nations Assembly and hit the place where he spoke but he never dared to pronounce and even less to execute a nuclear threat. It is necessary to highlight that the successors of Khrushchev ever also avoided making a direct threat of nuclear attack to United States not even in the worse moments of the Cold War.

Mao Tse Tung (1893-1976) never threatened with the use of nuclear weapons in spite of the intensity of the Korea and Vietnam wars in which China was involved directly because he was conscious that an atomic war was the humanity's end. The leaders of the western atomic power less, because obviously they were aware of the same thing.

For that reasons the North Korea threat of 2003 acquired so much relevance. It was an unprecedented political and military fact. It was not a threat with conventional weapons but a threat that could generate world chaos.

In synthesis, we can say that the 21st century has brought to the world a new reality: for first time a country threatens another to use its nuclear power. Although the threat per se is terrifying the cause of the threat is still more worrying. The country that threatens - North Korea- makes it in search of petroleum and food and uses the nuclear blackmail to try to get their material and political objectives.

NK doesn't have food but uses the third part of its GDP in military expenses

North Korea is an isolated country, without food for its population. It is a nation in which a very important part of their inhabitants must endure intense winters without heating because they don't have petroleum or any other sufficient energy sources. A country in which big housing buildings exist and there is not water because there is not electricity to pump; they can not use elevators for the same reason: there is not enough electricity. This means, a completely collapsed society. But, in spite of it, since 1998 they carried out tests to place a satellite in orbit, had the third more numerous army of the world -million and a half men- and the biggest force in commands of the world.

North Korea didn't have food but since the ninety-decade it had been devoted to produce missiles for the export that sells to the extremist governments of the world like a way of obtaining the foreign currencies that need.

Their communist allies of the past, China and the Former Soviet Union cannot give them now the economic neither energetic help in the same quantities that before they provided. China imports almost half of its necessities of petroleum and has had serious problems with its production of food and Russia confronts similar problems of food supply. North Korea doesn't have enough money to pay their imports. This fact difficult the international trade toward this country.

Starting from the breakup of the Soviet Union the North Korea economy began to feel the effects of the lack of attendance of that country and in the ninety years became visible the great crisis for lack of food. The decrease of the agricultural lands and natural phenomena as intense droughts and floods contributed to make more critical the situation. In the year 1995 North Korea was forced to request international help of emergency to get food. Since then confronts serious problems of food supply. The agricultural production, the energy production and the industrial production come falling simultaneously since the ninety years generating an intense economic and social crisis.

North Korea is one of the too few communist governments that stay alive in the world after the disappearance of the Soviet Union. Cuba and China are the other communist government that stills survives, but China has a special situation because has opened their economy to the Western market.

An old confrontation

The confrontations between North Korea and United States are not new. To have one idea about it, it is enough to remember the Korean War between 1950 and 1953. Those confrontations were part of the Cold War in which the Soviets as superior power always had the last word. But now the situation acquires a different character, since North Korea threatens a nuclear war autonomously. In the Cold War period the nuclear weapons control was in the hands of the Soviet Union and of the other four nuclear powers: United States, Great Britain, France and China. But the situation now has changed and the number of countries with tactical nuclear power (of short and medium range) has increased as well as the number of countries with strategic capacity (of long range); so that the world is in a new and difficult situation for the peace preservation.

Can North Korea shoot nuclear weapons against their neighbors and the United States?

With it own technological resources and the advice and material help of China and Russia, among other countries, North Korea has been able to develop an important atomic complex.

The reports disclosed in the first years of the 21st century by international analysts reveal that North Korea has a nuclear capacity offensive enough to destroy its neighbors South Korea and Japan and also that their intercontinental ballistic missiles, the Taepong II -with its heaviest load explosive- could reach the Hawaii Islands and Alaska and that with a lighter explosive load it could arrive to the rest of the continental territory of United States. This means that if North Korea is able to develop relatively light nuclear warheads it could affect the rest of the territory of United States directly through its intercontinental ballistic projectiles. But if is able to mobilize a launching platform toward the proximities of United States, as ships or submarines equipped with nuclear weapons, the threat would be even stronger. International analysts also assure that the MIG 23 airplanes of North Korea have the capacity to take and to use nuclear projectiles. If they find means of bringing near the proximity's of United States the MIG 23 or to buy or to get for any other means -as the donation- bombardiers with capacity to fly from a continent to another the situation would be quite difficult.

The Taepo Dong I is a projectile with a range between 1,500 and 2,000 kilometers whose tests North Korea carried out on the Japan Sea in several opportunities. The projectile Taepo II, also in test, could reach 6000 kilometers and reports assure that is being perfected to increase their radio of action.

Since the ninety years North Korea has come rehearsing the placement of a satellite in orbit. The reports indicate that still they have not been successful in that effort but that has won an important applicable experience to their intercontinental ballistic projectiles Taepo Dong II.

For beginning of the 21st century, the North Korean military force was composed of a million soldiers, 3000 tanks, 22 attack submarines, 500 combat airplanes, Scud rockets of Soviet production, rockets Nodong 1 of short and medium range built by themselves and the long range rockets Taepong 1 and 2 that come developing for some time. It is known that also has chemical and biological weapons. With all that military power is able to cause a great damage to their neighbors and depending on the range of their rockets or of the mobilization capacity that can obtain through ships, submarines or airplanes with enough flight autonomy able to be feed in the air could reach the rest of the Continent or of the world.

Another hypothesis considered by the international analysts is that North Korea could sell its nuclear weapons in the black market.

Is North Korea a real menace?

In October 2002, the Assistant of the Secretary of State of United States, James Kelly, visited the North Korea capital, Pyongyang, with a mission: to show to the authorities of that country the tests that United States had of the violation of the 1994 Treaty, through which North Korea committed itself not to continue its nuclear program and to eliminate it.

Confronting the group of proofs the North Korea government didn't have other alternative but confirming that, indeed, the country was carrying out nuclear tests for years in violation of the 1994 Treaty. Starting from that moment the international situation altered significantly and the same questions of the year 1994 arose again. Political analysts assure that in that period of time ---1994--- the president's Bill Clinton government had decided to carry out an attack against the nuclear facilities of North Korea, considering that these were a real threat for the security of the rest of the world. The attack was not carried out in that opportunity because inside United States arose dissident voices that promoted a negotiated peaceful solution. The former president Jimmy Carter was one of those influential voices. In that occasion Carter moved to Pyongyang and negotiated with the North Korea government the 1994 Agreement signed in Geneva the same year.

When in 1994 the President Bill Clinton governments decided carry out the attack to the Complex of Yongbion the situation was different to nowadays. In that moment perhaps the attack would have generated some relatively smaller effects because the complex was still in the formation stage and had not been able to develop completely. Anyway, still in the most conservative scenarios an attack of that type would have really generated serious damages in the Asia northeast and in Japan. The radioactive effects on all the near countries had been unpredictable besides the consequences of the reprisals that had surely adopted North Korea against their neighbors. There are historical examples of similar facts. On June 7 of 1981, for example, by means of an attack of its air force, Israel destroyed the place where began to settle the Iraqi nuclear reactor located in the area of Osirak at the north of Baghdad, attending of this way the reports of their intelligence services that considered that reactor as the center where Iraq would begin the production of atomic weapons. The attack didn't cause radioactive effects in the place because for that moment the reactor was not equipped with nuclear fuel.

The consequences of an attack now will be worse

Since 1994 North Korea has been able to consolidate their atomic power, in spite of the Agreement signed in Geneva. In 1994 a specific attack to the nuclear reactors of Yongbion perhaps had put end to the nuclear program of North Korea, but now is something late.

According to the reports disclosed by the specialized organisms, North Korea already has an important number of atomic weapons that could use toward near and distant objectives. This means that would be not only necessary to destroy the specific Yongbion nuclear center but would be necessary to locate and to destroy the atomic weapons that like is logical should not be localized in that complex but hide in sure places in different regions of that country. In consequence, an attack to the nuclear complex of Yongbion would not be enough because it could leave intact the destructive capacity of North Korea. In this case would be necessary to carry out attacks in diverse places that would imply the destruction of others parts of that country. But this would have some serious consequences. North Korea has a great military answer capacity. That power would respond immediately.

Ingenuousness

Was it an act of political ingenuousness to believe in the promise of the North Koreans leaders? The history shows too many examples of unfulfilled promises. For example, the British Prime Minister Arthur Chamberlain's (1937-1940) great error was to believe that he could negotiate with Mussolini and Hitler. His insistence in solving situations that could not be solved peacefully as the Spanish Civil War, the Mussolini's aggression against Ethiopia and Hitler's aspirations on the territories lost by the 1938 Munich Agreement offered all the advantages to those governments that took advantage of them and began the Second World War. The pacifist effort of Chamberlain didn't serve at all and in 1939 he had not other alternative but declaring the war to Germany under completely unfavorable conditions.

Three options and two hypotheses

Throughout time the United States and their allies has considered several alternatives:

a) To attack North Korea and Iran for destroying its nuclear power at any cost.

b) To negotiate a Treat of Peace for dismantles the nuclear facilities of North Korea and Iran.

c) Or to wait the development of the situation, making pressure through the United Nations.

First hypothesis: The former president of the United States, George Bush and some international analysts expressed in several opportunities that if United States doesn't destroy the nuclear facilities of North Korea and Iran, or do not negotiate a Treat of Peace with them, these countries could provoke the Third World War. According to the opinion of some analysts, North Korea could attack and destroy Japan and South Korea and in that moment surely will have the capacity to carry out a nuclear attack against United States, while Iran would make the same thing against Israel and Europe. This is one of the hypothesis that concern to the politicians and military leaders of the Western countries and for that reason they have requested to North Korea and Iran to abandon their nuclear programs. The hypothesis is based in the consideration of analogous situations in the history, but with a great difference: that now the nuclear power exists and in the past not.

Second hypothesis: The other possibility is that North Korea and Iran does not use their nuclear power for attacking their neighbors,

Europe nor United States.

The great problem is that a threat of nuclear war in any parts of the world it is, per se, a threat to the survival of the entire world.

North Korea doesn't have how expanding territorially

North Korea is chained of feet and hands with relation to any ambition of territorial expansion for solving their necessities of resources. China and Russia -their nearer neighbors- are much more powerful and could make disappear North Korea in few hours; for that reason North Korea doesn't have any possibility to annex neighboring territories except that invades South Korea, but in this country would find another power barrier like is the presence of United States. This reality places North Korea in a much more difficult situation. From where to obtain the natural resources that needs for their survival and that doesn't have in their territory? It does not have many alternatives. One would be to invade part of Manchuria but China would not forgive it and the other one to invade part of the Russian territory, but Russia neither would forgive it, so that the unique alternative is trying to penetrate -peacefully- South Korea, a country that has achieved a great cultural and material development. All this situation explains the great interest of North Korea in South Korea; because need South Korea to survive in the future. For avoiding the collapse, North Korea needs urgently petroleum and enhancing it food production capacity.

The atomic complex of Yongbion

In the year 1964 under Kim Il Sung[21] presidency in plenty Cold War, North Korea began it nuclear program with the construction of a reactor of 2 megawatt for the electricity generation with the support of the Soviet Union that trained the North Korea physiques. The reports of intelligence of those years highlighted that the reactor would not be able to produce the quantities of necessary plutonium to develop a program of atomic weapons.

In the seventy years with the same Soviet support North Korea began the construction of a second nuclear reactor of 5 megawatts for supposedly to increase the capacity of electricity generation. In 1987 completed this reactor that was able to produce 7 kilos of plutonium, enough for one or two nuclear bombs. But the time demonstrated that the true intention of North Korea was to produce atomic weapons in those reactors like has made and, indeed, in the eighty years began to manufacture plutonium in these reactors.

To build an atomic bomb are needed 5 kilos of plutonium approximately. It is known that the Yongbion reactor was closed in the year 1998 by two months, enough time to remove the plutonium contained in the reactor. It is known that from that combustible North Korea could have obtained approximately 30 kilos of plutonium, which would allow building 6 nuclear bombs. Besides their own capacity to produce plutonium and to enrich uranium for the production of atomic weapons, this country has bought important quantities of these products to Russia and China.

How much fuel has been able to process up to now is not known with accuracy but it is known that has developed enough quantities like to produce enough atomic weapons. Beside the two reactors, in the Complex of Yongbion exists a plant for the production of fuel of uranium of 100 tons per year. It is considered that this plant is able to produce much more, perhaps between 200 and 300 tons, which would be enough to feed the reactor of 5 mw and the two reactors that were in construction according to the 1994 Agreement.

Pressed by other countries that expressed great concern by the atomic program that was developing then, in December of 1985 North Korea signed with the International Atomic Energy Agency, IAEA, the Treaty of non Proliferation of Nuclear Weapons, but conditioned it to the retirement of the atomic weapons that United States had in South Korea. In September of the year 1991 the President George Bush announced the retirement of all the nuclear tactical weapons -of short and medium range- included the hundred weapons installed in South Korea. United States completed the demands although had never acquired a direct commitment with North Korea to dismantle its atomic weapons of South Korea, but rather that commitment was acquired directly by the IAEA and North Korea.

In 1991 both Koreas signed a treaty to eliminate the nuclear weapons in the Korea Peninsula and committed to accept mutual inspections to guarantee the execution of the agreement that prohibited proving, to take place, to receive, to accumulate or to use nuclear weapons.

North Korea acted secretly

But privately North Korea continued its program of nuclear weapons in spite of the commitments acquired with the IAEA and with South Korea. Indeed, in September of 1992 the inspectors of the IAEA discovered that there was a discrepancy among the reports of the initial program of North Korea and the quantity of plutonium processed that they find in that country and requests them an explanation. The IAEA requests an inspection in the deposits of nuclear material and it puts in evidence its suspicion that the country was violating the Agreement of No-proliferation of Nuclear Weapons signed in 1985. North Korea rejects this inspection and in March of 1993 announces its disposition of retiring of the Agreement of No-proliferation of Nuclear Weapons alleging reasons of national security. In April the IAEA declares that North Korea was not fulfilled the terms of the agreement.

After conversations with United States in June of 1993, North Korea suspended their decision of retiring of the Agreement and accepted the new requirements of the IAEA. In March of 1994 the IAEA inspectors arrived for the first inspection in one year. North Korea again rejected it and impeded the inspections in the Yongbyon reactor to the north Pyongyang and in May began to move away the nuclear fuel of the reactor of 5 megawats there installed with the obvious intention of producing plutonium.

The great political mistake of Carter

In June of 1994 the situation goes back again and North Korea announces its retreat of the IAEA again. After intense negotiations North Korea accepts the intervention of the former president Jimmy Carter and in October of 1994, after four months of negotiation, both countries signed the Geneva Agreement, by means of which North Korea committed to freeze and to eliminate their nuclear facilities and to allow the inspection of the IAEA inspectors. In exchange,

North Korea would receive two light water reactors, financed and builded for a consortium integrated by companies of United States, Japan and South Korea, the consortium KEDO and would also receive the petroleum and the food that needed. That is to say that Korea would solve its energy problems of short and medium term by means of the supply of petroleum and its problem of long term through the construction of the reactors that would guarantee its electricity necessities.

With that Agreement United States was making again -sixty years later- the same mistake that made with Japan in the thirty years, when gave to that country the petroleum, the iron and the steel that Japan used after to build the weapons and the planes to attack United States.

North Korea didn't comply the 1994 Treaty

Had hardly passed only four years of the Geneva Treaty signature when in December of 1998 again arise suspicions that North Korea had not fulfilled its commitment of freezing its program of atomic weapons and was disclosed the information that this country had a nuclear complex hidden in the Kumchang-ni area in the Pyongyang northeast. North Korea, as of habit, refuses the inspection of International Atomic Energy Agency, IAEA, but in May of 1999 announces that was willing to allow it in exchange for food. The inspectors went to the place and didn't find the looked for. Who did diffuse the report on Kumchang-ni? Why the IAEA gave credibility to the report since the beginning?

In November of 1999 the representatives of the consortium KEDO signed a contract with the Korea Electric Power Corporation to begin the construction of the two reactors of light water in the region of Kumho, in North Korea. This doesn't had logical explanation because the correct way was that to the first indication of the violation of the Geneva Agreement by North Korea, United States, Japan and South Korea had to stop the reactor construction; but they didn't make it and this error increased the crisis allowing North Korea to consolidate its position.

From the same moment that strengthens its nuclear program, North Korea began to use it like instrument to achieve political concessions, economic benefits and international help. "If you don't give me what I request I will use in the future my nuclear power" was the policy followed for North Korea since some years ago. In the 2003 said: "if you don't do my wish I am in capacity of using my atomic power."

Is very naive to believe in the word of enemies

The commitment of an enemy doesn't have any value. Hitler signed a non-aggression treaty with the Soviet Union but at the few time invaded the Soviet Union. Stalin is an example of the criminals of more cold blood of the world. During its government in the Soviet Union were made the biggest crimes and the neighboring countries knew of their ambition of power. In the year 1939 Stalin attacked Poland being distributed with Hitler the territory of this country. In that same year he appropriated on half of Finland and in 1940 appropriated of the Baltic Sea three republics. This means that Stalin and Hitler shared the same objectives, they were partners initially, but later Hitler betrayed him.

But Stalin's ambition didn't stop there. As consequence of the victory in the Second World War, Stalin had in the first times of the post war the control on part of Berlin. At the few time he established a new communist dictatorship government and a new country, the Eastern Germany giving beginning from that way to the Cold War. But he was not satisfied and simultaneously with this built the Communist Block, a group of countries governed by communist tyrants dependent of Moscow and integrated by Eastern Germany, Bulgary North Korea, Czechoslovakia, Red China, Albania, Hungary, Mongolia, Poland, Rumania, Tibet, North Vietnam and Yugoslavia, countries all dominated strongly, to blood and fire by the communists.

The conclusion is that the communists have always lied for obtaining their politics objectives. They were associated to the Nazis, invaded Finland, the others countries of the Baltic Sea and the Eastern Europe, caused the Korea war in the fifty years, the Vietnam war in those same years and later have had the hands put in all the 20 century conflicts.

Is not only naive but it also is incredibility

In the history of nations one can observe the conjugation of these two phenomena's. It is not only ingenuousness to believe in the opponent's good faith, but rather many times the attacked, the victims, they don't believe that their opponent has enough capacity to produce an aggression. That has happened many times in the history. For example, when North Korea began the construction of its first nuclear reactor in the sixty years said that it was only for peaceful ends -as producing electricity- and the other countries believed in them. But some time after was demonstrated that besides electricity the reactor would produce elements for nuclear weapons and, the most important thing, the training of the scientists for the later development of the atomic program.

In spite of the evidence that showed just the opposite and to the own declaration of North Korea threatening with nuclear weapons to their neighbors and United States, on May 15 2003, the Russian minister of atomic energy, Alexander Rumyantsev, declared in Moscow -in a meeting with the members of the International Committee of Physiques for the Nuclear War Prevention- that "independent observers have not registered any nuclear test in North Korea and that is not possible to speak of the use of nuclear weapons without making test of them..." However, international experts consider that Pakistan has carried out the tests for North Korea; this means that was Pakistan the country that helped North Korea to hide their nuclear tests.

Informs of intelligence disclosed in June 2003 assured also that Pakistan had provided to North Korea the centrifugal technology essential for the enrichment of uranium and, in consequence, for the production of atomic weapons. Pakistan's Scientifics worked directly in North Korea, among them the physical A.Q. Khan, considered as the creator of the atomic bomb of that country. Would be that the Russia minister of atomic energy ignored all these facts...?

Bush and the devil's triangle

In January 2002, after years of initiated the construction of the North Korea reactors, the President George Bush qualified Iran, Iraq and North Korea as the "devil's triangle" that threatened to the world with weapons of massive destruction.

In October 2002 after of verify the violation of the 1994 Treaty, United States decided to suspend -starting from December of that year- the shipping's of petroleum, of food and to paralyze the construction of the reactors for the electricity generation that were part of the 1994 Agreement.

In the same October, through their minister of External Affairs, North Korea admitted to possess the weapons and said that should have more nuclear arms to defend their sovereignty in front of the United States threat. The Korean minister requested United States a non-aggression pact and the commitment of not interfering in it economic development. North Korea radicalized its positions and in December of that same year rejected the inspections of the organism of atomic energy of the United Nations, expelled the inspectors and removed the observation equipment that the AEIA had installed in the nuclear complex of Yongbion. Since then, numerous versions that circulated to international scale assured that in the first years of the 2000 decade North Korea already was able to process enough plutonium to build an important number of atomic bombs and to enrich enough uranium with the same ends.

Atomic bombs for the next years?

Some reports assured that if North Korea starts again it reactor of 5 mw will be able to produce an atomic bomb annually starting from June 2003 and when completes the construction of the two reactors of 50 and of 200 mw -whose construction was temporarily suspended for the impasse with United States- will be able to build much more. Informs of the intelligence agencies highlight that when the Complex of Yongbion will be in full operation North Korea will be in capacity of preparing an important number of atomic bombs...Speculations? Truth?

North Korea and Iran will solve the problem of their missiles range

Surely, North Korea and Iran will solve the problem of their rockets range. If they have been able to develop the nuclear technology they will be able to develop rockets of long range. It is only a problem of timing because at medium term these countries will increase its technological capacity in this matter.

Smaller than New York

North Korea is a country of the Asia northeast, a country territorially smaller and with a little more population than the New York state. North Korea had 46,800 square miles of territory and 22.2 million inhabitants for the year 2002. The state of New York had 54,556 square miles of surface and 18.9 million of inhabitants for the year 2000.[22] For the year 2001 the GDP of North Korea was of hardly 15,500 million dollars, figure inferior to the GDP of the North

Dakota state that has the smallest GDP in United States. The GDP of North Dakota was of 17,757 million dollars for the year 2001.[23]

North Korea is a country without petroleum, with scarce reserves of coal that obtains their electricity (53%) of the hydroelectric source, but with serious supply flows that for long periods of time leave without electricity to complete regions of the country, because the generation capacity is insufficient and technologically behind. North Korea was a country with a foreign debt of $12 billion for the year 1996, debt almost equal to the GDP of the country in one year, with the added difficulty that most of the debt was in default. But, also, was a nation with an important deficit in their Balance of Payments, since for the year 2001 their exports of goods were of only $700 million, while their imports reached $1,600 billion, more than double of their exports.

A new conception of war

The conventional war is made by means of the occupation of territories and therefore is necessary to mobilize big quantities of men and equipment's. The atomic war doesn't need of anything of that. It is war of extermination in which everything is destroyed.

Only one nuclear submarine with its load of projectiles can destroy part of a continent. In the world there are hundreds of nuclear submarines equipped with hundreds of atomic missiles, besides the thousands of projectile existent in each one of the bases of the different countries possessors of nuclear weapons. This means something very simple: that man is really specie in real peril of extinction.

The help of China and the Soviet Union

Were the Soviet Union and China the countries that provided North Korea the means and the technical help to build their atomic weapons? Why did they make it? What advantages would they derive of it? Which disadvantages?

The Soviet Union and China always used North Korea as an instrument for the execution of their policies. North Korea has been the first barrier between Western and the Eastern Asia; barrier not only geographical but also politics and military, because in the Korean Peninsula there would be developed in a first instance any confrontation among the big superpowers in this side of the world. The military weakness of Japan and South Korea in front North Korea has always been very clear. The unique reason that up to now has stopped the action of North Korea toward their neighbors is the North American troops installed in those countries. Not for their volume that is relatively small - in South Korea there were only 37,000 North American soldiers - but for the consequences of an attack to the troops there parked, that would involve United States directly in the conflict. If those troops have not remained there, a long time ago North Korea had attacked South Korea and Japan.

North Korea and China have been allied by long time. In the Korea War of the fifty years China lost more than a million of soldiers and Mao Tse Tung said that China and North Korea were as the lips and the teeth. This alliance has changed for political and economic reasons but it is not known certainly until where. In spite of the situation generated by the natural resources crisis of China, international experts consider that North Korea receives at least half of the external help budget of that country.

From where does North Korea obtain its technology for the nuclear development and of missiles systems? International analysts assure that it has been proven that China has sold North Korea an important quantity of uranium that this country has been enriching in its nuclear complexes. Those international sources say also that it has been proven that Chinese companies have sold advanced military technologies to North Korea and countries of the Middle East like Iran. The same thing has made Russian companies.

These facts demonstrate that there is not an entirely sincere rhetoric among the great powers. China the same as Russia assures to have taken measures to avoid the illegal sales of atomic weapons and projectiles of long reach, but the certain fact is that in countries like North Korea and Iran appear new technologies that supposedly come from those countries. Informs assure that China has sold North Korea not only one great quantity of high-strength uranium, an essential substance used in the equipment's for the enrichment of the uranium, but also other important materials and products. It is also known that North Korea has acquired a great quantity of plutonium coming from Russia and that the Former Soviet Union provided them the technology for the production of its missiles of short, medium and large range.

United States has criticized the Chinese government and the Russian government for not having made all the necessary to impede the sale of illegal weapons but these countries allege that they have taken the preventive measures. Until where is this certain only the time will say. So far, there is a real fact and it is that countries like North Korea, India and Pakistan possess nuclear weapons, while Iran is working for obtaining them.

The North Korea food crisis

The centralized communist economy has not been able to guarantee the food to the population. For the year 2002 North Korea was nine years old facing an intense shortage of food as consequence of the deterioration of its agricultural lands for droughts and floods, besides problems due to the lack of fertilizers and fuels for production; this accentuated the problems of health and malnutrition of the population's placing it in a truly difficult situation.

North Korea was always a dependent country of the Soviet Union and China, which provided good part of the petroleum and the foods that consumed. But with the disappearance of the Soviet Union the situation changed and North Korea did not receive more that important support. Something similar but lesser intense has happened with the help of China, country that has lost a good part of its capacity of food producing. Indeed, China has come diminishing its productive capacity in sustained form as consequence of natural phenomena and of the wrong use of the earth resources because of the growing contamination.

In 1994 the China reserves of food began to shrink generating a serious crisis in North Korea. Millions of people suffered the lack of food. The situation was so serious that the North Korea government was forced to request food like international humanitarian help in

1995. International informs disclosed then highlighted that thousands of families roamed by the capital, Pyongyang, by other cities and by the frontier with China in search of food.

The lack of food has stayed in the time increasing the social crisis at the extreme that for the year 2001 United States, South Korea and the European Union gave more than US $ 300 million in direct alimentary help, besides the aim of the United Nations organisms. In spite of this serious crisis, North Korea for that same year dedicated 31.3 percent from its Gross Domestic Product to military expenses.

Stalin used hunger to dominate his enemies

It is not the first time that a communist country faces serious problems of food supply. In 1933 the Soviet Union, under Joseph Stalin tyranny, suffered a severe crisis for lack of food and there are authors that think that this crisis was not a fortuitous fact but rather it was impelled, created by Stalin's government with ends of to diminish and to control the population that didn't support him or of whose support doubted. This means that the communist government used hunger like weapon to murder part of the Soviet Union population.

Similar facts took place in the 20th Century in other communist countries as Mongolia in the same thirty years, in North Vietnam between 1955 and 1956 in China between 1959 and 1961 and in Cambodia between 1975 and 1979, in times of the Khmer Rouge.

An isolated diplomatic country

North Korea has diplomatic relationships with too few countries of the world. Established a permanent mission in the United Nations but doesn't have diplomatic relationships with United States, for example. Maintains commercial relationships with too few countries too, among them China, Russia, Japan, Singapore, South Korea and Hong Kong.

The country exports mineral products, metallurgists, agricultural and fishing products and some manufactured goods including armaments and imports petroleum, cereals, coke, machineries, equipment's and goods of consumption.

By lack of water China might become a grain importer

Asia -the most populated continent of the world- suffers the consequences of the earth resources overexploitation. A clear example of it is what happens with the underground waters and the China Rivers that irrigate good part of the agricultural lands. Those sources of water present a process of exhaustion that put in danger the agricultural production and might transform at China into an importer of food, specifically grains, since won't be able to satisfy its population's demand. This phenomenon already began to be observed in the Chinese society and was one of the reasons that motivated in 1995 to diminish its exports of grains toward North Korea. When China interrupted the sale of grains to North Korea this country didn't have another alternative but requesting international help to the United Nations.

A restitution of sufficient help in food to North Korea by China seems not very probable since this country continues confronting serious production problems derived of the shortage of the most important inputs for the agricultural production as water. An example is what happens in the Yellow River that had lost their flow and already doesn't reach the sea. In the year 1996 the River was dry during 133 days while in 1997 remained dry during 226 days. The County of Shandong is the last route of the river before arriving to the sea. This county produces good part of the corn and of the wheat and it has been seriously affected as consequence of the river drought

What happens with the Yellow River also passes with other important rivers of China and with the more and more scarce underground sources of water. It is considered that China has around of 50,000 kilometers of rivers of certain magnitude and 80% of them are degraded and are not capable for the fishing, due to the contamination that receives. The Yellow River, for example, is polluted of heavy metals and other toxic matters that impede its use for human consumption and irrigation in good part of its route.

The decrease of the China capacity for producing food will generate an important impact in the world economy, since will look that food in the international markets causing the increase of their prices. The poor countries are not in capacity of resisting an increment in the price of the food, they would not have how to pay the new prices and, in consequence, they would be in front of a true problem of survival. If the countries with more population as China and India diminish their food production capacity, the world situation will be aggravate since the cereals world reserves have diminished significantly in the last years. India, the other giant of the world suffers a similar situation and should use very important part of the energy that produce to pump water of the underground.

World experts have estimated that China would have not enough water at medium term; this means that would have to import an important part of its food. What will do then?

To produce one kilo of wheat are needed 1000 liters of water

As water is every day scarcer the food shall be also scarcer in many regions of the world. To produce one ton of wheat are required a thousand tons of water. This means that to produce one kilo of wheat is needed 1000 liters of water. To produce one kilo of chicken are needed two kilos of cereals that is to say, two thousand liters of water, while to produce one kilo of pig are needed four kilos of cereals that is to say four thousand liters of water.

In the measure in that the population grows, the consumption of food increases too and, in consequence, the consumption of water that is the basic input for production. If the availability of water diminishes, the production of food diminishes. If this happens the food prices will increase and every day fewer sectors will satisfy their needs.

China neither has enough petroleum

A similar situation occurs regarding the oil. China has not been able to increase their reserves that remained static in 24 thousand million barrels from the year 1989 until 2000. In that same period the production passed from 2.8 million barrels to 3.2 million barrels, an increment of 14.2 percent. But is the consumption the one that presents the most impressive figures. Indeed, between 1990 and

2000 the consumption rose from 2.1 million daily barrels to 4.6 million daily barrels, an increase of more than 100 percent.[24] The projections of the China consumption for the first twenty years of the XXI century reveals that this country will increase its consumption from 3.5 million barrels for 1997 to 9.5 million barrels for the year 2020, more than twice in the signal period.[25]

This has generated serious problems to North Korea for obtaining the oil that before China sold them. For that reason in the 1994 year generated the nuclear crisis that culminated with the signature of the Geneva Agreement by means of which United States committed to give the petroleum that required. It is necessary to highlight that North Korea consumed 80 thousand daily barrels of petroleum for the 2000 year that imported totally and that had for that same year a refinement capacity of 71 thousand daily barrels.

Peace cannot be bought

Nicolas Machiavelli, [26] author of "The Prince", one of the most read political books in all the times, said that is an error to believe that the peace or the good wishes of who considered us their enemies could be bought. And that asseveration is a great truth. Two examples confirm this thesis of Machiavelli: Before the Second War the United States gave a great help to Japan and too few time after Japan attacked the United States. During the Second World War and in the post war the United States helped the Soviet Union but they didn't thank that help and, on the contrary, immediately provoked the Cold War. There are many examples of this kind in history. What mechanism does impel this human attitude? Correspond to the experts in human behavior to explain it, but the real fact is that ingratitude is something common in the international policy.

The oil and nuclear help

During years the United States had supplied part of the petroleum that North Korea consumes. Also, as consequence of the Geneve Agreement of 1994, the United States, South Korea and Japan began to build two nuclear power stations for producing electricity in North Korea.

The time demonstrated that North Korea didn't comply their part in the Agreement. To build a nuclear plant to an enemy is something absurd. It is as to give to your enemy a double-barreled shotgun. If you give to your enemy a new powerful arm you may be sure that he will threat you with that new arm and if it is necessary will use the new weapon against you.

North Korea took advantage of the whole time lapsed between 1994 and the year 2002 to assure the continuation -undercover- of its nuclear program but, meanwhile, received the petroleum, the food and the technical and financial help of U.S, Japan and South Korea for the construction of the two promised nuclear power stations.

Was in October 2002 -eight years later- when the authorities of the International Atomic Energy Agency and United States become aware that North Korea had unfulfilled its part of the Agreement of 1994. Starting from that moment they decided to suspend the shipment of petroleum and to suspend the construction of the conventional nuclear plants. But it was already late. For that moment North Korea already had an arsenal of nuclear weapons and projectiles.

A similar situation to what happened between the United States and North Korea happened before the Second World War between the United States and Japan

When one examines the world history and compare facts happened in different times realize that there is a trend to the repetition of history.

In the first years of the 20th century Japan began a process of important economic and military rebirth that highlighted among all the countries of Asia. But Japan was a country with a great weakness: didn't have raw materials, especially petroleum, the new energy that began to occupy the first place in the world. But hadn't other fundamental raw materials as iron, coal, neither the steel, key elements for the industrial development and the sustenance of an important warlike industry. In search of those raw materials, in the thirty years Japan invades Manchuria. There establishes an important colonial enclave. But Manchuria was not enough since in this region there was not petroleum; therefore looked in the distance toward China and toward the Eastern Indies dominated then by Holland, places where there was enough petroleum.

For the development of their economic activity Japan imported from United States good part of the raw materials and intermediate goods that consumed. Petroleum, iron, steel, but it also imported gasoline, motors for airplanes and airplanes, besides other many goods and equipment's. Practically Japan didn't have petroleum since only produced less of 10 percent of its consumption and their airplanes, its fleet, their trucks and tanks of war was fed with petroleum. United States was the main supplier of petroleum of Japan and supplied more than two thirds of the petroleum that consumed. Was also its main supplier of iron scrap and steel that after Japanese transformed in intermediate products or in finished goods. So that the Japan armed forces were armed forces dependent of the petroleum, motors, iron and steel that United States provided them. Certain sector of the Japanese leadership was humiliated by these facts, especially sectors of the Japanese army that sought to have a much more decisive position in Asia and in the world.

In their expansionary purpose in search of raw materials, essentially, Japan takes a new step: decides to invade China on August of 1937. Starting from that moment begins a war against an unarmed population that is slaughtered cruelly by Japanese. The objective was to obtain in the continent the natural resources that could not obtain in its territory formed by a group of islands. The Japan armed forces made genocide against the China's population. The North American population rejected the aggression and demanded to its government not continue selling petroleum, gasoline and the airplanes with which was slaughtering the Chinese nation. But the government of President's Franklin Roosevelt did not adopt the measures that demanded him most of the country and United States continued providing petroleum and equipment's to Japan. [27]

So began the aggressive action of Japan in the thirty years, action that will complete later with its direct attack to United States in Pearl

Harbor the seven day of December 1942.

The war with Japan: a lesson of history

The hostility of certain important sectors of Japan against United States was evident since the twenty years. But as well as there were hostile sectors there was also who wanted the peace. The history of the disagreements between ones and others is the same history of the war. Those who was in favor of the war executed all kinds of ambushes trying to murder those moderate leaders that was in favor of the peace included the Prime Minister, plot that was discovered in July 1940. As consequence of this situation a new Prime Minister was designated: the Prince Konoye. In this reorganization of the cabinet enters as War Minister the general Hideki Tojo, well-known with the nickname of "Kamisori" that meant "The knife of shaving", a warlike with a dark past able to develop all kinds of intrigues, like demonstrated its military record.

The Japanese government was in that time a mixture of extremist positions and of moderate ideas. The Emperor maintained an eclectic position. The Prime Minister Konoye maintained a similar position but showed a bigger inclination toward the peace because was aware of the Japan weakness, position that other leaders shared, even military bosses of great prestige like the admiral Isoroku Yamamoto, chief of the Japanese navy. But Yamamoto was a disciplined military willing to accept the orders that were imparted and in spite of not be accord with the war, was he who directed the military operation of attack to Pearl Harbor.

The Prime Minister Konori until the last moment, October 1941-that is to say, until 6 weeks before the attack to Pearl Harbor- tried to avoid the war. Konori proposed a meeting with the North American President Franklin Roosevelt but the Secretary of State of then, Cordell Hull impeded it, adducing formalisms. The history remembers that Cordell Hull said then that was not accord with the meeting between the two leaders, because the Japanese premier had not made a formal application through the diplomatic channels. For that stupidity of Cordell Hull the United States and Japan lost their last opportunity to avoid the war.

As consequence of their failure in reaching the meeting, the Prime Minister Konori left his position on October 18, 1942 and was replaced by the warlike General Hideki Tojo ---Kamisori--- an enemy of peace. Too few weeks after, on December 7, 1941, the Japanese Army attacked Pearl Harbor.

Hull is in fact the great one historical responsible of the war on the part of United States, while "Kamisori" is the great one responsible on the part of Japan. Hull believed to know everything. Was determined in a pacifist attitude and he didn't saw that the Japanese radical sectors clearly wanted to cause the war. Hull never believed that Japan would attack United States in spite of the evidences that showed the Japanese preparations. The foul attitude of Hull together the violence of "Kamisori" provoked the Pacific War, one of the bloodiest of history. Hull, as Secretary of State, didn't make the necessary to avoid that United States followed proportionate petroleum, gasoline, iron, steel, motors, airplanes and other equipment's to Japan, in spite of the situation of visible conflict that existed among the two nations. And, as before was said, to crown it all, when at the last moment the Japanese Prime Minister tried to speak personally with the President Roosevelt, Hull opposed, alleging that the Japanese Prime Minister had not requested the interview for the ordinary diplomatic channels. And, of course, few days after what Hull didn't wait took place: Pearl Harbor.

Chapter 8

Aggressors exists because the victim accepts the aggression

"If by a visible cowardice you grant something to another person, that person will not stop there. He will want much more...But if having discovered your enemy's intentions quickly you prepares to point your forces against him, he begins to be considered with you, still when your forces are inferior to his forces"... The quote belongs to The Prince[28] a classic of the political literature written in the XVI Century.

Fearing to face the war in two fronts, in Europe and in Asia, during years the President Roosevelt consented to the demands of Japan and continued selling petroleum and the rest of the raw materials and equipment's that they needed.

Roosevelt thought that the negative of the United States to provide petroleum to Japan would provoke the invasion by Japan to the Eastern Indies governed by Holland where petroleum existed in abundance. Japan took advantage of all the material supplies of United States and got ready for the war. And, at the end, the consideration towards Japanese had not none sense because Japan equally attacked. If they had not received the petroleum and the raw materials that during so much time United States provided them perhaps the history has been different and the horror of that war had been avoided.

The aggressors attack because the victims accept the aggression. Shark, that is a terrible animal that can destroy any other marine animal, doesn't dare to attack dolphins that, without having the force that have sharks, have another much more important thing: the value and the cunning to face them. The felines, in spite of their sagacity and their voracity respect elephants because they know very well that although elephant doesn't have the teeth that has a tiger, elephants has the force and the courage to squash them.

There are non-rational men. These types of men are in essence animals and therefore they conserve the instincts of the wild animals. They demonstrates this clearly when assume violent attitudes. In that moment they overcome the attitude of wildest animals. It is enough only to observe the outrages made in the wars that have been in the entire world in all the times to check the truthfulness of these arguments. The wild beasts only feel respect for other animals when they know that those other wild beasts can return the same damage or to cause them one bigger.

If all men were really rational, balanced and just, violence would not exist in the world; the conflicts would be solved in a peaceful, reasonable way, by mean of dialogue and cooperation. But, regrettably this isn't truth. As well as there are reasonable and peaceful men there are irrational and violent and the only way that they respect is threatening them with the force or using the force against them. To this category belong the tyrants and fanatics.

The fanatics, the disturbed, are who provoke war

Only a personality outside of the normal can provoke a war. The balanced, normal men don't cause conflicts; they live in peace and appreciate peace. A man inwardly balanced evaluates the damage that will cause his decisions to the population and, of course, avoids causing any type of sufferings but the tyrants and the fanatics no. This class of personalities enjoys doing wrong. For example, in what class of mind could be conceived a slaughter like the committed against the Jewish during the Second World War? What class of mind could conceive and to build Auschwitz and the other Nazi concentration fields where they take until to defenseless children? What class of mind can use gases against a poor and unarmed town, as make Mussolini in Africa and Saddam Hussein against the Kurdish population in the eighty years?

It is not necessary to go very far in history to find characters that have harmed humanity. In the 20th Century Lenin, Hitler, Mussolini, Stalin is a good example of the human cruelty. They were state bosses but in turn they were sick mental that had arrived to the power. Characters that enjoyed the suffering of the other persons and on the name of concepts like the homeland and the population they justified their crimes.

These characters have always existed in all the moments of history. But the modern world has today the possibility to know them, to notice its intentions on time and to adopt the measures to neutralize them and to take them out of the power. The development of the modern media, the existence of the communication for satellites an now Internet allows that any event in any part of the world can be known by the rest of the citizen's worldwide in the same moment in what happen. There is not place in the world to which the television cannot arrive. This fact had a great importance because it allows to the world to be alert and to adopt the necessary measures to avoid that those tyrants, fanatics and lunatics can make unpunished acts against the life and the humanity's security.

Mission of the centers for strategic studies

The leaders of the democratic countries have the obligation of granting to the prospective and strategic studies a much more important place. Nobody can know what can happen in the future accurately but an appropriate forecast system can contribute to see the possible scenarios and to get ready for them. A leader is a person that can see in the present what is invisible, the things that remains hidden for most. A leader is a person able to anticipate the future in intuitive form but also in rational form, by means of the application of the scientific analysis method. A leader identifies a situation, observes, examines it in their relationships with the other situations and formulates hypothesis based on his proper knowledge and in the historical experience. This should be the main mission of the political and strategic studies centers: to anticipate to what can happen in the future and to present the alternatives to prevent the big problems of the future.

Errors of the political leadership lead to the war

When Hitler began his aggression against Czechoslovakia and Poland the other countries didn't make anything. But at the few time he attacked the Eastern Europe countries, the Nordic countries, France, England, until finally attacked to the Soviet Union, in spite of the Non Aggression Pact signed between Hitler and Stalin.

If when Hitler took the first steps in his strategy of war the world had faced him, is very probable that the history has been different. In the case of the Pacific War one mistaken appreciation of the reality on part of United States leaders, the overestimate of the own force and the underestimate of the Japan forces created the conditions for the war. If the President Roosevelt and the Secretary of State Cordell Hull had seen the situation in different form, probably the war would be avoided. Were the political errors of the Secretary of State Hull, especially, those that determined the war and its bloody development? If since the first moment that the Japan leaders began to give samples of hostility the United States had faced them not selling more petroleum, neither steel, iron, airplanes, motors, gasoline and all the rest of products that sold them, Japan had not accumulated the power to attack later United States.

The 21st Century world has to guarantee its survival protecting of the unbalanced and fanatics that can provoke a nuclear war. Anywhere that this danger exists should be eliminated at any cost because is preferable the sacrifice of some few than the sacrifice of humanity's.

Does the Catholic Church believe in the Apocalypse?

In ovals located in the walls of the Sixtin Chapel in the Vatican appear the figures of the different pontiffs. A tourist that visited the place in the ninety years commented me that got powerfully its attention that was only three empty ovals in the place. One of them will correspond to the Pope John Paul II, Carol Woytila and, in consequence, lack to stuff only two ovals after Woytila. And she asked to the Vatican guides why in the gallery there were only three empty places and not more. The guides responded that the legend say that will come only two pontiffs after Woytila. And, in consequence, that it will be the time before the end of the world; fantasy? reality?

The answer of the Vatican guides coincides with the expressed by the prophecy of Saint Malachy[29] who conceived hundred twelve mottos (slogans) that would correspond to the different pontiffs starting from the Pope Celestine II. The last two slogans for the conclusion of the prophecy are the number 111 "De Labore Solis" that means "of the sun work" and that supposedly correspond to the Pope John Paul II.

The following slogan and last would correspond to the successor of Woytila, the pontiff number 112 that supposedly will have as motto "Gloria Olivae" that means "the glory of the olive tree". The experts consider that there are some significant coincidences. The two most relevant are that, indeed, the successor of Woytila, Pope Benedict XVI was born a Saturday of Glory and the olives identify the Order of the Benedictines.

Considering this is true, then we are in the presence of the last Pope from Saint Malachy list.[30]

To culminate their papal prophecies Saint Malachy says that:

> "During the final persecution of the Holy Roman Church, the seat will be occupied by Peter the Roman, who will feed his sheep in many tribulations; and when these things are finished, the seven-hilled city will be destroyed, and the formidable Judge will judge his people. The End. [31]

Some interpreters consider that with John Paul II began the finally of times. And that starting from that moment an antichrist will come (Apocalypse XII). These interpreters consider that could be a rebel Pope. According to this interpretation the legitimate Pope would be Peter Roman. But Peter Roman would not be the last Pope of history because the end of history is not the end of the world in physical terms. According to those interpreters, the end of history means the end of the times of lack of faith, the end of a time and the conversion of the Jewish people to Christ. In that moment the Popes as the first Pope, Saint Peter, that was Palestinian, will return to Jerusalem; fantasy? reality?

Recent documents were found in Europe which are attributed to Nostradamus who assured that between the years 1992 and 2012 the final confrontation among the Christianity and the Islam will be fulfilled and that struggle would lead to the Apocalypses...

According with this prophecy, in this period the Anti Christ would appear, the Christian Church would be strongly affected and the Pope would transfer the Church settlement from Rome towards a more secure place.[32] The prophecy, would assure that in the year

2012 a cosmic phenomenon would occur that happens only every 13,000 years; the last one happened thousands of years before of Christ. This phenomenon would indicate the end of history; the experts assure that symbols of this prophecy are also expressed in the walls of Saint Michel of the Revelations Church in France; church that was built by the Templars...Fantasy... Reality?

Will the nuclear weapons generate the Apocalypse?

Until 1945 man had not developed a destructive capacity the sufficiently big as to destroy the world. But starting from that year, when he knew and used the atomic energy as weapon of massive destruction, the situation changed. Now man with all the destructive power that has created could finish the life in the earth.

The accumulated nuclear power is of such magnitude that is impossible to understand it in all its significance. There have always been big events of the nature that have generated destruction, but in form partially in specific areas of the planet. But about a total destruction of the planet in the past only exist few hypothesis like the Universal Flood and the hypothesis that sustain the current scientists about the great devastation happened as consequence of the crash of a huge meteorite against the earth, fact that would have caused the destruction of the most ways of life existent in that time, among them the dinosaurs and other big species. The destruction created by the collision of the meteorite against the earth was of such magnitude that is compared to what could produce today a nuclear hecatomb. This means that the man, with the weapons that has created, could generate today destruction similar to the generated by the nature when the great meteorite collided with the earth and put end to the dinosaurs and the other forms of life.

The destructive power of the nuclear weapons is not a fantasy. That power of the nuclear weapons can put end to the earth in only too few minutes: to finish with a continent, a complete region, a city, depending on the quantity of energy that is used. According to the Theory of the Relativity (Einstein 1905) *each body possesses an own energy similar to the product of its mass expressed in grams by the square of the speed of the light in centimeters per second. If it is destroyed a gram of matter completely by the energy irradiation would be liberated a quantity of heat of 20.000 million kilocalories that could warm 200.000 tons of water from 0° until the temperature of boil of 100° centigrade; this shows clearly that the matter constitutes a fabulous reserve of energy.*[33] For that reason, one can meditate perfectly on facts as the implicit one the figures of the pontiffs in the Vatican. Why are there three empty ovals and not four, five, ten or twenty? Is it only because there is not enough physical space in the Sixtin Chapel? This is a fact that opens the doors to all the possibilities of the doubts and the imagination. But the fact that doesn't admit any type of doubts is the great danger that represents for humanity the arsenal of accumulated atomic weapons, an arsenal that in hands of any unbalanced, of any fanatic could generate a great world disaster, the Apocalypse.[34]

So far, the big nuclear powers, United States, the Former Soviet Union and now Russia, France, Great Britain and China -that are part of the Security Council of the United Nations- have used sensible and carefully their nuclear power. Starting from the end of the Second World War and up to 1991 when was dissolved the Soviet Union there were moments of great tension like the crisis of Berlin in 1948, when the Russian commandant -obviously obeying orders of Joseph Stalin, the Soviet premier - decided to close the terrestrial accesses to the city to impede that the supplies and the allied troops had access to the city.

Also very difficult moments were those generated by the rockets crisis in Cuba in 1962, but the rationality was always imposed and any type of nuclear incident was avoided. In every year there were wars with the direct participation of the big nuclear powers. But all those conflicts were developed with conventional weapons being avoided the use of atomic weapons. Now the situation has begun to change and the possession of atomic weapons is no longer only in hands of the five big world powers. Countries governed by radical leaders and religious fanatics have been able to possess nuclear weapons and other elements of massive destruction as biological and chemical weapons.

The Doomsday Clock

An interesting idea can be found in the following report of DPA in January 2007, which informed that the Clock of the Final Judgment, "Doomsday Clock," was advanced two minutes. The Clock of the Final Judgment was created in 1947, to show to what distance in the time is humanity of a nuclear war. The clock was created two years after Hiroshima and

Nagasaki. At the moment at which it began to work, the clock marked seven minutes before the twelve.

Through time the clock has been adjusted following the worldwide situation. The closest that the clock has been of the twelfth hour was in 1953, after the tests with hydrogen bombs made by the United States and the Soviet Union, then the clock was only two minutes for twelve.

When the Cold War finished in the Eighties the clock returned to be to seven minutes to twelve and thus it remained for years, but the on January 17 of 2007, the Bulletin of the Atomic Science magazine, in charge of the clock, announced that it had gone ahead two minutes, that is to say, that the clock was at that moment at five minutes to twelve and they justified the advance because of the dangers represented by the atomic programs of North Korea and Iran for the world peace.

Chapter 9

Philosophical principle of change

The societies are live bodies and, in consequence, they comply an evolutionary cycle that is to say that it born, grow, reproduce and die to begin ever a new cycle. None society remains static, anchored to a certain way of life. The societies constantly change, and that change is fed by the natural tendency of man to the search of the new. Still in the most traditional and attached to the past societies, the change is manifested in constant form. The modern society, the cybernetic society of the 21st century is a very eloquent example of the permanent change. All the values considered traditional have suffered deep transformations in the last decades of the 20 century and at the beginning of the 21st century. The family -as institution- suffers a deep change. The marriage like main center of the social life has weakened and in its place has appeared new non formal forms of union; in some countries and regions -as the County of Ontario in Canada[35]- has even arrived to accept something inconceivable until hardly little time ago, like the marriage among people of the same sex. The religious faith has also suffered its setbacks and man has become more materialistic, transforming the lucre and wealth into his new religion. Globalization, as economic doctrine, has made their appearance in the world scene, increasing the differences between the rich countries and the poor countries.

The history of the world is characterized by the existence of centers of power in every period, centers of power that exercised their domain since the military, political, economic, scientific, social, cultural and religious point of view. But the characteristic common to all the times is that those centers of power have moved in systematic form. Has not been eternal power. All the centers of power have experienced the evolutionary cycle of birth, splendor and death to begin a new cycle. The Former Mesopotamia, Egypt, the Hellenic Civilization, the Roman Empire, the Spanish Empire, the Portuguese Empire, the French Empire, the German Empire, the English Empire, the Japanese Empire, the Soviet Empire, all have known the ascent and the fall.

Starting from the breakup of the Soviet Union in the year 1991 the

United States remains as the principal military and economic power of the world. For how long more will continue being it? Is it possible the eternal power?

The history of the world teaches that none human power is eternal, that the big powers stop, leave to be it and that are displaced by new powers. Is this a law of history?

If the world peace stays, China looks like the emergent power of the 21st century. Although militarily China is still to dozens of years of distance of United States, its potential of military and economic development should not be underestimated since in few years it could become the power that competes with United States.

Importance of the animosity feeling and of the hostile intention

Carl Von Clausewitz, [36] general and Prussian theoretical military whose book, *Art and Science of the War* has been considered a classic on the matter, said that the conflict between men depends on two different elements: the animosity feeling and the hostile intention. And he affirmed that the feeling of more inflamed, wilder and almost more instinctive hate is inconceivable if it is exempt of hostile intentions.

In the modern world, the mass media, press, radio and television, especially, determine in a good part the feelings and opinions of the population. The messages of the leadership through the media are something very important. The spread of negative news, of words of hate, or, in contrary, of positive news, of words of happiness and solidarity exert a deep effect on the population.

So that we can say that in the modern world, because of the development of the mass media, the transmission of feelings of animosity to the population is one of the most important cause that determine the hostility of a country toward other country.

West doesn't feel animosity for North Korea

The people of North America and Europe don't have feelings of animosity toward North Korea. It is more; the common citizen perhaps doesn't know where exactly North Korea is. The Western mass media usually do not express negative concepts on the population of the countries that appear in contradiction with Western. On the contrary, reports of the specialized agencies assure that the North Korea official press speaks frequently of barbarism acts supposedly made by North American military forces in the Korea War of the fifty years an that even exist a Museum of Terror where are presented examples of those acts; as it is obvious, this contributes to increase the animosity toward United States.

Orientals people don't fear death

The mentality of the suicides is incomprehensible and incredible for any normal person. For that reason costs so much to understand and to believe that this class of people can take ahead its terrorist plans. But the suicides, the fanatics exist. They are everywhere, especially the fanatics moved by religious and racial beliefs. The Japanese kamikazes during the Second World War may be one of the best examples of the fanaticism. These aviators shattered their airplanes against the North American ships to guarantee in that way the success and the destruction of their objectives.

During the II World War, Japanese kamikazes didn't matter to die because according to its religious beliefs to die for the Emperor was an act of heroism. The Oriental Culture -among them the Muslims- believe in the life beyond the life, in the life after the death. Are people willing to die, people that accept the death like a form of personal realization and of service to the Emperor or the religion that profess. That conception of life gives to these people an advantage in the war, because they don't fear die or they fear in a smaller proportion. So that anything of stranger would have that a radical leader of the eastern countries -that include the Middle East- can provoke the Third World War, because is people that considers death like something sublime, people that believe that dying for religious cause or politics will give them grace in the sky and eternally.

Cultural confrontation

What is in game in the world is the great cultural confrontation between the Eastern Culture and the Western Culture; the confrontation among the Judeo-Christian vision that dominates the Western World and the majority Eastern conceptions, the Islamism, Buddhism, Taoism and Confucianism, among others.

The religions of the Eastern Culture are the religions that profess the most people of the world because in those continents also lives most of the world population, and is arriving the moment of the great cultural confrontation among those two big ways of to see and to act in the world.

Every day the Eastern Countries acquire a more important presence in the Western World. The economy of the Asian countries has in the 21st century and had a great importance in the last years of the 20 Century creating new markets that have given an important impulse to the trade and the world economy as a whole. Although Japan is an allied country of United States and of Western is important don't forget that Japan is an Eastern country, a country of Eastern culture that in its moment -in the Second World War- had an open confrontation, a war with United States. Although those wounds have been closed and Japan is today one of the Seven Big industrial powers beside the Western Powers, Japan continues being and it will continue being a country of Eastern culture. And Japan is today one of the main economies of the world. The economies of the Eastern Countries that include the Middle East would dominate the world economy if they act as a whole. Asia and Africa concentrates the 73 percent of the world population's. The production of Asia -included the Middle East- represents a very important part of the world economy and it will follow being in the future.

The importance that has acquired Asia in the world economy is demonstrated by the investments carried out in the last years of the 20 Century and beginnings of the 21st century in the region. China, for example, received in 1996 a third part of the whole investment of the Third World. For the year 2001 the total volume of imports and exports of China overcame the $500 trillion, jumping this country of the twentieth eighth place in 1978 to the sixth place of the world trade in the year 2001, after United States, Germany, Japan, France and Great Britain. For the year 2002 a report of the World Trade Organization assured that China had become the fourth exporter of the world after United States, the European Union and Japan. For the same year 2002 China overcame the $50 trillion dollars of foreign investment becoming the most important international receiver of investments for that year.

On December 11 2002 China incorporated to the World Trade Organization. In the previous period to their entrance to that organization began to receive an important flow of capitals that see in the Chinese market a great expansion potential. And, indeed, it has been true, as demonstrate the facts since immediately increased their exports to be located in fourth place like world exporter as it was already explained.

Only China and India have more than the third part of the world population's. So that an opening of these markets that goes accompanied by an increment of the purchase capacity of the populations' of those countries would have an important impact in the world economy. One of the most important effects will be on the consumption of food, since up to now the populations of those countries have had a low level of income. This will generate a new situation in the world demand of food since China and India are confronting for some years serious problems with their agricultural production due to the lack of water and pollution.

China is one of the biggest countries in the world. Has 9.6 million square kilometers of surface approximately and also the most population with approximately 1.254 million inhabitants for 1999. Although formally their government is communist, his economy is not it and starting from 1978 began a series of reformations that they have allowed to reach the place that today occupies in the world economy. A country of those dimensions is obviously an economic power. Their work force was only of approximately 689 million people for the year 1999. While their international reserves reached to 114,399 million dollars for the year 2002, one of the most important of the world.[37]   For the year 2006 China occupied the second place -- after Japan -- in matter of international reserves as may be verified in the table 2.

India is the other great giant of Asia with economy market, but a country of Eastern culture that preserves its traditional way of live. There is in the Asian continent other nation of great economic importance, South Korea, a country of market economy that has accepted the Western economic pattern but that culturally it has always been a country of the East that conserves its traditional way of life, their customs.

Up to now East and West have cohabited in relative harmony. The conflicts between East and West could be bigger. In the 20th Century highlight the war between Japan and United States in the Second World War, the Korea war with active participation of the United States and the Vietnam War. Other warlike events as the wars in the Middle East, the Gulf War, Afghanistan and the war against Iraq have convulsed that region.

If are looked the causes for of each one of these conflicts, will be proven that there is a fact common to all them: the economic difficulties of the countries. In the forty years, Japan lived a difficult economic situation. In that time, Korea and Vietnam were countries that confronted equally serious economic problems when the war begins in both countries. The Palestinian problem is not only a politics-territorial problem but also an economic fact of survival because this people lost the geo economic space where lived and worked. The problem of other minorities as the Kurdish people slaughtered by Saddam Hussein, the situation of the Chechens in their confrontation with Russia, the case of the Afghanistan people, among others, puts in evidence that the economic issue, the survival, the production and the work are determining and decisive factors of the peace. It cannot have peace without economic justice, without employment, without possibility of producing.

But each population, each nationality -in a wide sense, that is to say, as cultural manifestation- has their proper customs and difficultly accepts the ways of life of others populations. Mc Donald settled in China but respecting the local customs and that it has been an entire success. Other populations have been less permeable to the foreign influence. The Islamic fundamentalist countries are an example of it.

Can the cultural confrontation leading to the political confrontation and this to war?

The specialists in war consider that the opposition, the contradiction between the objectives of the states is one of the principal reasons that lead to war. Why does a human being have go to murder another?

The conflict between the human beings born when somebody seeks to usurp or to remove to other person something that the other considers proper: something material or a right, a privilege. The old war was a war for the conquest of territories, for obtaining economic advantages, but the modern war no longer has only that motivation. It is not only the territorial disputes but also the threat that represent a country or a group of countries to other countries a cause of the modern war.

With the development of the modern ballistic systems a country can threaten another to thousands of kilometers of distance. It is no longer the proximity, the fight for borders, the struggle for to conquer territories in other places the decisive cause of the modern war. Now the question is much more complex, because any country can develop the scientific and technological capacity to build weapons of massive destruction and to use those weapons to thousands of kilometers.

The United States was the first country in developing the power of the atom with military ends. Continued the way the big powers, the Soviet Union, England, France and China. But now other countries also possess atomic weapons. They are Israel, India, Pakistan, Iran and North Korea. So that anything of stranger would have that in a period of too few years the atomic weapons become the conventional weapons and that today's conventional weapons becomes the warlike scrap of the future. For example, North Korea has argued that has decided to develop its nuclear power as a form of to eliminate part of its conventional armed forces and to save money.

Chapter 10

The confrontation with the Islamic Fundamentalism

Since that was created the state of Israel in 1948 the confrontation between Arab and Jews acquired a new and more intense dimension. Until the first years of the 21st century the conflict in very few occasions had surpassed the frontiers of the Middle East like when in the seventy years Arab fanatics made attacks in the Olympic Games in Germany or the kidnapping of the OPEC minister in Vienna in those same years. But the situation has changed and proves of these are the terrorist attacks of September 11 2001 in New York and Washington, since this is the first time that United States suffers an attack in its own territory as consequence of the Middle East confrontation.

A direct effect of these facts was the invasion of Afghanistan by United States in the following months to the attacks. Another consequence was also the invasion of Iraq by United States in the year 2003. These facts although have consolidated the North American presence in Asia have also accentuated the hostility of the Islamic nations toward the United States. There are countries like Pakistan, Syria and Saudi Arabia whose governments maintained in the past a balanced attitude, but they face the reactions of their people. Until where would resist the governments the pressure of its own people? Until where does exists animosity between the Islamic fundamentalism and others Asian countries toward United States? What do you think?

Prepares Iran atomic weapons?

Iran always has assured that its nuclear program is only for peaceful ends, for the electricity generation. This fact gets the attention because Iran is one of the first world oil countries and perfectly could use petroleum to cover their energy necessities instead of using nuclear energy. Some experts consider that it is not justified that Iran -having petroleum in abundance- uses the nuclear energy to generate electricity and for these reason is logical to think that behind the project exists the real intention of using the atomic facilities to build weapons. Today, internationals analysts consider that Iran is one of the countries that seriously threaten the Middle East peace and the world peace because of its intention of to built nuclear weapons.

It should not be forgotten that was in Iran where took place one of the most important revolution against Western at the end of the seventy years. Starting from then was established in that country a theocratic regime and the confrontation with Western were radicalized.

In those years (1979) the ayatollahs revolution triumphed in Iran, and a fundamentalist religious group headed by the ayatollah Jomeini overthrew the Sha Rezha Palevi who governed Iran since the year 1953. The ayatollahs argued that the Sha had westernized the country and they considered this like enough cause for its overthrow. The relationships among the two countries passed by moments of great tension like the generated by the invasion of the North American embassy by crowds directed by the Jomeini's government, which took as hostages to 63 officials from United States and maintained them kidnapped during fifteen months inside the embassy. From the same moment in that the fundamentalist priests took the power, Iran maintained a confrontation attitude with the United States.

In June 2003 -and in front of the evidence presented by the international community- Iran didn't have alternative but recognizing finally that was building two nuclear plants, which had maintained secretly until that moment. Nuclear experts consider that the plants are in capacity of generating nuclear fuels for the production of weapons. In one of the plants of heavy water located in the region of Arak they are developing nuclear fuel, the plutonium that is used in the production of nuclear bombs. In the other plant -located in the region from Natanz to the south of Arak- that had remained secretly until June 2003, Iran builds a plant for the enrichment of uranium, that the same as the plutonium, is used in the production of nuclear bombs.

Iran comes working its nuclear program privately for years. The International Atomic Energy Agency, IAEA, knew the official program -the plant of Bushehr built for Russia- for peaceful use of the nuclear energy, specifically the electricity production. But the experts consider that, in parallel, Iran had come maintaining a hidden program as the same authorities of that country have recognized. It is known, for example, that Iran didn't report to the International Atomic Energy Agency, IAEA that in the year 1991 bought to China 1.8 metric tons of natural uranium, which deposited in the Teheran

Laboratory of Investigation. Why China, as seller of the uranium, didn't notify to the International Atomic Energy Agency, IAEA, as was its duty?

Unofficial reports highlight that besides the plant of Bushehr and of the plants of Arak and Natanz exists other secret nuclear facilities that work actively. In the region, other countries also have nuclear weapons, among them Pakistan and India that maintain an old border dispute. The great danger is that these neighboring countries can use their atomic power one against the other.

Iran wants to play in the Major Leagues of the international policy and with that intention President Mahmud Ahmadineyad announced on February 11, 2008, in the acts of the 29 commemoration of anniversary of the Islamic Revolution that, by the summer of 2008, his country would launch to the space two rockets for telecommunications made with their own technology.

In the act, celebrated in the Azade Square, in Teheran, the Iranian President assured that they already had launched a first research rocket successfully and hopes to continue the space program.

If this information is true, this means that Iran already owns the capacity to send missiles to a great distance, that is to say, that it could reach Europe and the United States when it totally develops its nuclear capacity.

Iran has been increasing its military budget in a sustained form the Nineties as it can be appraised in the following table.

Table 9
Islamic Republic of Iran
Military Expenditure in constant (2005) US $ millions

Years	US $ millions
1995	2,351
1996	2,659
1997	2,977
1998	3,142
1999	4,374
2000	6,695
2001	7,408
2002	5,981
2003	7,013
2004	7,892
2005	9,057
2006	9,849

Source: Information from the Stockholm International Peace Research Institute,
SIPRI, URL, address.

The nuclear power of Israel other threat to the peace

The balance of Asia and the Middle East depends also of another country with a nuclear consolidated power; it is Israel, which has achieved an important development of atomic weapons, according with qualified analysts.

International sources assure that Israel has increased not only their terrestrial forces with nuclear weapons but also its naval power, by means of the acquisition of a submarine force capable also of taking also atomic weapons.

Israel is a key point for the peace of the Middle East and Asia. The clash with its Arabic neighbors is permanent and a solution is not glimpsed. In the moment, the visible hypothesis of nuclear conflict in the Middle East is between Iran and Israel but it might be extended to others Arabic nations in the future. It will depend on the facilities that have other Arabic nations to acquire the nuclear knowledge. As this is feasible and can be acquired with money, it is perfectly possible that in the second decade of the years 2000 other Arabic nations possess the atomic technology.

In Israel as in the Arabic nations there exist extremist, fanatical sectors inclined by the war. If these sectors are imposed, the possibilities of peace in the region will weaken much more and the danger of nuclear clash in the area will be increased.

Chapter 11

The threat of nuclear war didn't disappear with the breakup of the URSS

Good part of the world has lived the illusion that the nuclear threat disappeared as consequence of the dissolution of the Soviet Union, but this is not true. Reports of the Western intelligence estimate that for June 2003 Russia possessed 18,000 nuclear heads in their arsenal of weapons of which are operative weapons more than 8 thousand. For the moment of its breakup the Soviet Union had 35,000 atomic bombs approximately. Of being certain the estimates of the Western intelligence agencies that arsenal has decreased in half, but that it is an enough quantity to destroy the whole humanity. However, there are facts worthy of being outstanding. One of them is that Russia continues the production of its nuclear weapons in spite of having dismantled half of them. Why does it? Which is the reason? According to reports published by the intelligence agencies, Russia had settled as a priority in its military budget of the year 2003 the construction of the nuclear missiles SS27, the calls Topol-M. It is also known that Russia has continued the tests of other nuclear projectiles as the call SS-19, proves carried out from the Space Center of Baikonur in December 2002, missiles that impacted in the Peninsula of Kamchatha. Before, in October of the same 2002 proved their missiles SS-25 from the city of Plestek. This has a meaning and it is that Russia has not stopped to modernize its nuclear arsenal whose power, in spite of its reduction remains intact. Proves of these is that for the year 2001 were the second country with the biggest military expense in the world, 60,000 million dollars.

For the year 2006, Russia had a military budget of US$ 49,500 the fourth between the powers. Since the decade of the ninety years, Russia has increased in a sustained form their military expenditures.

Russia will be always a mystery. So far, their new leaders have looked the way to the democracy, the economic progress and the peace. If they achieve it, the democracy in Russia will strengthen. The Russian people will check that the democracy is better than the communism and the extremist tendencies that still fight for a return to the past will weaken or will extinguish. But if they don't achieve it, the risk of the return of sectors that don't believe in the democracy will exist. If this happen the world could return to the stages of the Cold War but now in the 21st century. The life doesn't regress. It always evolves. But the Western democracies should be attentive to give the Russian democratic leaders the necessary help so that they can consolidate the democracy in Russia, and it is sustained, essentially, in the economic strengthen.

China, the emergent power

China is a military power. It possesses the nuclear technology since the sixty years. In October 1964 proved with success its first atomic bomb. Two years later, in October of 1966, shot their first guided missile with a nuclear load and in June of 1967 proved their first bomb of hydrogen. So that the military capacity of China it is not in doubt. Which is the power of its strategic force of missiles, called the Second Artillery? None person can explain this with accuracy, but it is obvious that the Second Artillery is an important force. The military budget of China of 42,000 million dollars was the third more big of the world for the year 2001. China is one of the five members of the United Nations Council Security with veto capacity. Is member of the International Organization of Atomic Energy, member of the Treaty of Not Proliferation of Nuclear Weapons and has agreed with United States a moratorium in the tests of atomic weapons. But, in reality, many of these agreements are not fulfilled. China, for example, has continued giving technical and material attendance to Pakistan in their nuclear program providing missiles M-11. It is known that China collaborated with North Korea and with Iran to who sold chemical weapons. Why would not sell nuclear weapons and technology? For this reason United States imposed commercial sanctions to several Chinese entities. On the other hand,

China criticized United States for to sell weapons to Taiwan.

The military power doesn't depend in decisive form of the scientific and technological capacity; it depends too on the disposition of the inputs to manufacture what man thinks. But among all the resources the most important is money because with money a country can to buy the whole technology and the weapons that want.

Russia, Israel, Great Britain and France have armed to China

In the eighty years and to help China to stop its powerful neighbor ambitions, the Soviet Union, the Western countries as Great Britain, France and Israel gave military attendance to China. As a consequence of the Tiananmen massacre United States and the European Union decided to impose a seizure to China and not selling more weapons to this country. But the seizure didn't last a lot. Israel -country aligned to Western- never accepted it and the rest of the Europe countries began progressively to sell again their weapons to China. As consequence of this, in the ninety years China was able to modernize its obsolete military equipment's and to acquire technology of first order.

China has not only bought to the European countries but also to Russia after the disappearance of the Soviet Union in 1991 acquiring important equipment's and advanced military systems as technology for the development of intercontinental ballistic rockets. The system of intercontinental ballistic rockets has a range capacity of 5000 and 8000 kilometers and both can arrive to the continental territory of United States.

China has also obtained of Russia submarines armed of nuclear projectiles of long range type Victor II and the technology for its construction, bombardiers of long range and airplanes with tanks systems for its supplying in the air. Russia has also provided China more than 250 airplanes of the type Sukhoi-27, a version similar to the North American F5.

It is known that China is one of the best clients of Israel that has sold military aeronautical technology, missiles and another series of sophisticated equipment's. The same thing has made France and Great Britain that sold China advanced radar equipment and competed with Israel and Russia to provide China the airplanes of type Awac. The China market of weapons is the more coveted by the international sellers of weapons because this country has been able to accumulate the enough financial wealth to acquire as much as wants in military matter.

The governments from Western countries have allowed that the industries of those countries make military business with China without thinking on the political consequences and in the consequences that for their own security implies the sale of that technology and equipment's. The military strengthen of China breaks the balance of power not only in Asia but also in the entire world and the responsible for this are the countries that have armed to China. The Western countries have made again the same error that once United States made when armed to Japan before the Second World War. The same thing would happen with China. With the same weapons and technology that the Western country has sold them, China would put of knee to the Western countries by means of the use of the weapons or with the simple threat of using them.

The nations that have sold weapons to China have acted only as merchants without consider the political consequences. With the purpose of obtaining a gain those countries have given --to a country that is obviously a potential enemy-- the weapons that would threat them in the future. Who can guarantee that won't be of this way? Is somebody able to assure that China won't use in the future the military power that has acquired in the Western countries to threat at the same Western? International sources assure that up to now, the naval power recently acquired, guarantees to China -at medium term- the domain of the Western Pacific, the Asia South East and the China Sea.

China is then the great challenge for the Western countries. North Korea is an intermediate stage of the process, a real phase, obviously, a phase that could destroy an important part of the East of Asia and of the Western countries, but China is, really, the big shark that is behind the sardine that is North Korea.

United States is the first power

In spite of the power of the other countries, United States continues being the first power, their military budget of US $ 396 for the year 2001 were biggest of the entire world.[38] This figure represented more than six times the military budget of Russia, more than nine times the budget of China, more than nine times the budget of Japan and more than ten times the military budget of the United Kingdom for the same year.

For the year 2006, the military budget of United States reached US$ 528,692 millions, the most important of the world. The wars in Afghanistan and Iraq have determined the military constant growth of the United States military budgets since the year 2001.

The atomic power of United States is of thousands of intercontinental ballistic missiles, dozens of atomic submarines, hundreds of bombardiers of long range with capacity to use nuclear weapons. A really terrify force.

The dollar is the most important strategic resource of United States

The economic and military power of The United States has its more important expression in the dollar. The United States has an immense financial capacity, because as consequence of its economic power, the dollar is the international instrument of change most accepted until now; this allows US, with their proper currency, to satisfy all its needs of internal and external financing. The United States does not have to resort to the currency of another country to acquire any thing on the international markets. It is enough to United States simply to pay with its own currency that is accepted in the entire world. This strengthens the US financial capacity and provides a financial autonomy that the great majority of countries do not have. While other countries must go in search of hard currency -of international acceptance- as the dollar, the pound sterling, the Euro or the Japanese yen to realize its international payments, The United States with its proper currency can acquire what wish in any part of the world.

While other countries have to resort to the *external debt,* it means to debt in foreign currencies, especially dollars, the United States don't need foreign currency for financing its deficit; this means that can finance its deficit through of *internal debt.*[39]

Until the 30s decade was the Sterling pound the currency of major world acceptance, because it was the currency of the Empire that was dominating the world. In the post war, in 1945, was created the International Monetary Fund that adopted the dollar of the United States as the currency for the international transactions and the new value that substituted gold as instrument of international reserves of the countries.

According to the new international rules created in 1945, the issuance or emission of national currency in each country must be based in the amount of international reserves and, as already was mentioned, the main instrument of reserves is the dollar of the United States; this is other reason that explains why the United States is the first economic power of the world.

Throughout the time, the dollar has passed for several crisis and other currencies has obtained a significant position in the international markets among them the German Marc and the Japanese Yen; in the first decade of the 21st century a new currency appeared in the world, the Euro, that reflect the new economic power of Europe. In spite of it important value, the Euro has not been able to substitute the dollar in the international transactions. Conversely, the strengthens of the Euro has favored the United States position in the international markets, and attracting new commerce flows toward the United States because it is less expensive to buy in the United States than to buy in Europe.

In the year 2007 the United States requested to China appreciating their currency, the Yuan, in 15% in regard to the dollar; the monetarist authorities of China accepted to appreciate the Yuan in an inferior scale and this fact has helped to improve the balance of payment of the United States, making most competitive the North American products for other countries.

At medium term it not seems feasible the substitution of the dollar by other currency for the international transactions, in spite of the important economic growth of China. Hardly in too few years, especially since the first years of the 21st century, China won a new important space in the world economy. For example, between the year 1995 and the year 2005, in ten years, China multiplied by 1,100% their international reserves passing for US $75,357 million to US $821,513 million. After Japan, China had for the year 2005 the most amounts of international reserves.

Table 10
International Liquidity, International Reserves minus Gold, Millions of US$,
End of Period, 1995-2005

Years	Japan	China	Russia	United States Billions US$	Germany	United Kingdom Billions US$	France
1995	183,250	75,377	14,382	74.78	85,008	42.02	26,853
1996	216,648	107,039	11,276	64.04	83,178	39.90	26,796
1997	219,648	142,762	12,894	58.91	77,587	32.32	30,927
1998	215,471	149,188	7,801	70.71	74,024	32.21	44,312
1999	286,916	157,728	8,457	60.50	61,039	33.30	39,701
2000	354,902	168,278	24,264	56.60	56,890	38.77	37,039
2001	395,155	215,605	32,542	57.63	51,408	34.19	31,740
2002	461,180	291,128	44,053	67.96	51,171	37.55	28,365
2003	663,289	408,151	73,174	74.89	50,694	38.48	30,186
2004	833,891	614,500	120,808	75.89	48,823	40.69	35,314
2005	834,275	821,514	175,891	54.08	45,140	38.48	27,753

Source: International Monetary Fund, 2006 Yearbook, International Statistics,
pages 223, 298, 308, 365, 509, 605, 608.

The concept of power is something integral; for to be a power, a country must having economic, technologic, scientist and military strengthens. The money let to buy a good part of those elements. The countries that have more money have the possibility of obtaining the military power that the want. Especially, because after the breakout of the Soviet Union in 1989, the market of arms changed in the world because this country become in an important supplier of the Third World countries in this matter.

Japan: an ally from Western countries

Japan has been always a country with vocation of power. As was proven in the previous table, Japan was the country with the most international reserves for the year 2005 and this fact became its currency, the yen, in one of the first of the world and revealed the great potential of this country. In parallel, if Japan develop and consolidate their military capacity, the world balance of power will change in an intense form.

As consequence of the Second World War treaties, Japan and Germany were handicapped of developing an arms career. To almost sixty years of their defeat in the year 1945, Japan shines now as the country with the third military budget of the world, since for the year 2001 dedicated 40,400 million dollars to its defense expenses. This represents double the military budget of Germany that had assigned 21,000 million dollars for that same year. Their neighbor threatening presence, North Korea, compel to Japan to perfect their defense systems, this necessarily implies to get ready to confront the nuclear, chemical and biological power of North Korea.

Japan has the scientific and technological capacity for the development of nuclear weapons. Reports highlight that has a complete system by means of which the fuel is burned in a special type of reactor and recycled in another type of fuel in an infinite way without necessity of adding fresh fuel. In a part of this process plutonium takes place and burns again. Japan diminished its source of electricity generation through the hydroelectric system from 15.4 percent in 1980 to 8.7 percent in 1997. And its dependence of the petroleum for the electricity generation diminished from 46.2 percent to only 18.2 percent during the mentioned years. On the other hand, Japan increased their use of coal from 9.6 to 19.1

percent. And their nuclear generation from 14.4 to 31 percent in the signal years that is to say that duplicated the use of the coal and the nuclear energy.[40]

So far, what have prevented to Asia to exercise a more significant paper in the world have been the contradictions among their different countries: the historic differences among China and Japan, among China and South Korea, between China and South Vietnam, among China and India, between China and the Former Soviet Union, between China and Hong Kong, China and Taiwan. In all those years China has been in the center of the conflicts for action or for omission, as aggressor or as victim.

The economic leadership of the Asian continent has been exercised until the first years of the 21st century by Japan that is one of the first economic powers of the world, but China acquires every day a bigger importance. In the near future China and Japan will dispute the economic leadership of that great continent. If is solved the difficult situation with conflicting countries as North Korea the most important states in Asia like China and Japan might coincide since the economic point of view and the creation of an Asian common market would not be an utopia. It could be a reality in a future. This would give to the new currency that would arise of that common market a very important paper. That might be the new currency that could compete with the dollar and with the euro in the future.

Until where the interests of Japan and China could coincide is the great question. Until where can the cultural identity to influence for the creation of a new economic alliance between China and Japan?

Will be forever Japan an economic ally from the Western countries?

The paradox: the poorest countries are those that threaten the world peace

India was the country that had the biggest military budget among the emergent nuclear powers. For the year 2001 India had foreseen a military expense of US $ 15.6 billion, 3.3 percent of its gross internal product, which was of 459 billion dollars for the year 2000. Iran had a military budget of US $ 9.1 billion in the year 2001 that represented 8.5 percent of its GDP of US $ 107 billion for the year 2000. After we find Pakistan that for the year 2001 assigned US $ 2.6 billion to their military budget that represented 4.2 percent of their GDP of US $ 61billion for the year 2000, Iraq, with US $ 1.4 billion and North Korea, with US $ 1.3 billion of military budget for the 2001.[41]

Weapons and nuclear systems can be bought in the black market

Although it seems the topic of a fiction movie, it is not as seems. Certainly, nuclear weapons can be bought in the black market. According to the reports of experts in the matter, it is possible to acquire complete missiles or part of missiles to be assembled. It is possible also to get the capacity to shoot them at long distance, that is to say, the vehicles with intercontinental ballistic capacity. This means that a country doesn't have to possess the technological neither scientific capacity but the money to acquire this weapons.

Another concern of the authorities of the Western countries is the increase of the number of countries with capacity to deploy ballistic missiles since mobile surfaces as ships. For example, a report of the Institute for Strategic Studies from 2008, assures that "the China People's Liberation Army Navy is acquiring new types of nuclear and conventional submarines." The report says, moreover, that in January 2007 "China made a test of anti-satellite missile that reveals the modernization efforts in this case on developments in missile guidance, command and control..."[42]

If only a part of the military budget would be used to produce employment and food the world would be a better place

If all the countries -and especially the rich countries- would make an effort in this sense the situation of the world would be different. The levels of poverty would diminish and the human beings in most of the world would have a worthier life.

The money dedicated to military matter certainly exercises a multiplier effect on the world economy but the result of that production doesn't generate happiness to the world. Each projectile, each bomb, each tank of war, each combat airplane, ship of war or submarine what represents is death and sadness. And instead of this, the production should have a superior end as to create happiness to the human beings. Instead of manufacturing weapons the world should dedicate those resources to the scientific and technological investigation to diminish the negative effects that generates the human activity on the environment. Instead of manufacturing weapons the human beings should use those resources in generating employments in the agriculture, in the industry, in tourism, in health and in education, in the invigoration of the family like basic institution of the society, in the teaching of the traditional values as morality, the respect to the other people's right, honesty, in guaranteeing all the children of the world a home, an appropriate feeding, the medications and medical cares that require.

Table 11
Military Expenditure in constant (2005) US $ millions

Years	United States	United Kingdom	France	China	Japan	Germany
1995	357,382	50,818	53,100	15,000	42,471	43,238
1996	337,946	50,554	51,738	16,600	43,328	42,395
1997	336,185	48,276	51,926	16,800	43,521	40,854
1998	328,611	47,691	50,535	19,300	43,405	40,993
1999	329,421	47,529	50,979	21,600	43,483	41,822
2000	342,172	47,778	50,395	23,800	43,802	41,147
2001	344,932	48,760	50,225	28,000	44,275	40,474
2002	387,303	50,949	51,257	33,100	44,725	40,604
2003	440,813	57,452	52,643	36,600	44,814	40,044
2004	480,451	60,234	54,018	40,300	44,473	38,816
2005	504,638	60,076	52,917	44,300	44,165	38,060
2006	528,692	59,213	53,091	49,500	43,701	36,984

Source: Information from the Stockholm International Peace Research Institute, SIPRI, URL, address.

The figures do not need any comment; they reveal how the world misses the opportunity of building a better quality of life.

To guarantee peace is necessary to prepare for peace, not for war

To guarantee peace it is not necessary to get ready for war. To guarantee the peace is necessary to make all the necessary to guarantee peace. It is the culture of the peace the one that can guarantee the peace. Not the culture of war the one that can guarantee the peace.

Conclusion

The future of the world peace will be decided in the Middle East and Asia. In this region will be felt with more force the first impacts of the natural resources shortage: water, food and petroleum. The Middle East and Asia concentrates the countries that until the moment –first decades of the 21st century - seek to strength its nuclear power. These countries are Iran, Syria, India, Israel, North Korea and Pakistan. To those countries is added China already a nuclear consolidated power since a lot of time. Except for Israel, the other countries before mentioned have political and economic objectives opposed to the objectives of the Western nations and especially of the United States.

China fights for to become the dominant nation of Asia and the world. So far, China has intervened in all the conflicts that have occur in the continent since the culmination of the Second World War. China participated actively in the Korea War of the fifty years, too in the Vietnam War in the fifty, sixty and seventeen years. China has achieved important political and economic concessions of their neighbors' and of the rest of the world.

The politic and economic counterbalance of China in the Asian continent is Japan, a country that has adopted the capitalist economic pattern with success. Japan is also becoming a military power because of the threat of its neighbor, North Korea, that doesn't lose opportunity to execute provocation acts, as the test of missiles on the Japan Sea regularly.

In the Asian continent there are also other areas of great tension like Syria, Afghanistan and Iraq; the confrontation among India and Pakistan and the difficult economic crisis that live the Republics of the Former Soviet Union as Kazakhstan, Uzbekistan, Turkmenistan and Tajikistan, in many of which remains part of the Soviet nuclear power.

The lack of natural resources as water, food and petroleum is the weakness of most of the nations of this continent and base of the conflicts. This is demonstrated by the history and this situation has not changed. North Korea is a good example, a country that has threatened its neighbors and United States with the use of its nuclear power. Since the ninety years North Korea lives a severe crisis of foods and energy that forced to this country to request international help in 1995. This situation has stayed and it has been intensified with the pass of the time placing North Korea in a desperate situation.

But a solution is not glimpsed for the problems of natural resources of the Asian continent neither of the world since, on the contrary, everyday that passes the drought is bigger in diverse parts of the planet, the underground water reserves are drained or contaminated and, in consequence, everyday is smaller the quantity of available water to assist the growing necessities of the agriculture, the industry and the domestic use. More than half of the 600 cities of China already confront severe problems of water. Other countries of the region confront the same problems that everyday are increased. It has provoked a substantial decrease of the agricultural production. The experts of United Nations calculate that China will increase its population from 1,200 to 1,500 million inhabitants between the year 2000 and the year 2030. This increment is superior to the current total population of United States. The reserves of petroleum in the world are not increasing and what the technology can make to use the resource more efficiently is still limited. The fracking, the new technology of the second decade of the 21st century would be not sufficient to satisfy the needs of the countries that are employing these technical. The contamination and the global warming as consequence of the increment of the fossil fuels in the atmosphere, the nuclear tests, the wrong use of the garbage in diverse regions of the world, aggravate the situation of the natural resources.

The world population will increase approximately a third among the years 2000 and 2030 passing from 6 thousand to 8 thousand million inhabitants. The consequences of this fact on the world necessities of water, food and petroleum cannot be measured at this time with accuracy. Any projection is imprecise. But what is sure is that is a gigantic quantity that the scarce natural resources won't probably be able to contribute. The fight for the natural resources will be then the more important characteristic of the world politics and the economy in the 21st century.

The perspectives of peace are weak because in spite of the commitment of good part of the nations of not stimulating the development of nuclear weapons, that commitment in reality is not fulfilled and every day more countries begin to produce this type of weapons.

There is not sincerity in the words of many countries that proclaim peace. Some international organizations recommend using the word risk instead of the world threat, but in the 21st century we face a reality: the threat of some countries that set in peril the world peace.

The North Korea threat is insignificant in front of the true threat that China represents. China is a country that every day consolidates its nuclear and economic power, but their natural resources every day are scarcer. How will make then to obtain them?

Japan is one of the countries of more revenues[43] and wealth of the world and of Asia, but neither has natural resources. How will make to obtain them when in the future they begin to be every day scarcer? How will be the struggle for the scarce resources?

Will dominate the Eastern countries to the Western countries? What do you think?

Everything will depend especially on government's type that arises in the different countries of the world in the future, especially, of the governments of the countries that have nuclear weapons. If arise democratic, balanced governments, there will be peace. If conversely, in these countries take the power extremist or political and religious fanatics the situation will change totally and the risk and threat of local and global conflict will be increased. With the existence of the atomic weapons only God can avoid the Apocalypse.

God bless and save the world.

Quotes

It is necessary to remember that this is not something new in the North American economy. A similar setting was already seen during the Great Depression of the twenties and thirties in the 20th century.

2 http://pablorafaelgonzalez.blogspot.com

3 Harry Elmer Barnes. *Historia de la Economía del Mundo Occidental, Unión Editorial Hispanoamericana.* Mexico. 1973, pages 622-623.

[4] Idem, page 624.

[5] Earth Policy Institute, March 7, 2007. "Water Prices Rising Worldwide," by Edwin H. Clark II
http://www.earth-policy.org/updates/2007/updated 64.htm

[6] Energy Information Administration Annual Energy Review 2006 table 8, 10 page 257.

[7] Department of Defense of the United States of America Annual Report to Congress 2008, Military Power of the People's Republic of China. Page 1.

[8] Idem page 24.

9 www.exxonmobil.com/corporate/energy_outlook..aspx The Outlook for Energy: A view to 2030.

[10] U.S Energy Department. Energy Information Administration

11 http://pablorafaelgonzalez.blogspot.com

12 AQUASTAT FAO 2005 2nd UN World Water Development Report 2006, "Water a shared responsibility", page 123.

13 Centre for Defence Information, Washington, http://www.cdi.org/program/index.cfm?programid=1

14 2nd UN World Water Development Report 2006, "Water a shared responsibility," page 120.

[15] World Resources Institute. Earth Trends August 2006 Monthly Update: Water Scarcity. http://earthtrends.wri.org/updates/node/73 by Tom Damassa. Friday September 1 2006.

[16] Pablo Rafael Gonzalez. Running Out: How Global Shortages Change the Economic Paradigm, page 1 Algora Publishing, New York, 2005

17 OPEC Annual Statistical Bulletin 2000

18 Estimations of the United Nations specialized agencies, consider that for the 2030 year the world population will be increased in a third approximately in relation to the existing for the beginning of the 2000 year. To attend to the new world population will be necessary to increase the food production in 60 per cent, for which will be necessary, in turn, to increase the agriculture of irrigation. This, like is obvious, implies the utilization of a major quantity of water. But this resource is becoming exhausted in good part of the world. For the 2050 year the estimations of the United Nations World Population Prospects 2002 calculates that the world population will grow almost in 42 per cent in relation to the existing population in the year 2003 and that it will pass from 6,301 to 8,919 million inhabitants in the notable period.

19 This continent is not only suffering the intensive destruction of its rivers as consequences of intense droughts and increasing pollution but, besides, is extracting of its underground sources (fountains) more waters of what these sources (fountains) in natural form can recover. The same thing happens in other regions of the world.

[20]Asia was sheltering 60 per cent of the world population for the year 2003 and Africa 13 per cent. Source: United Nations World Population Prospects 2002.

21 Field Marshall of North Korea army (1912-1994) was president of this country from 1948 up to his death, when was replaced by his son Kim Il Jong, who continues governing the country.

22 Source: U.S. Census Bureau, Census 2000

23 Source: U.S. Department of Commerce. U.S. Bureau of Economic Analysis, Millions of chained (1996) dollars.

24 Source: OPEC Annual Statistical Bulletin 2000

25 Source: Energy Information Administration, Administration International Energy, Outlook 2000

26 Politician, writer and Italian philosopher, Florence 1469-1527, author of The Prince.

27 One of the best studies on the origin of the war with Japan is the work of Dr. Daniel Yergin, in his book *La Historia del Petróleo*, (Javier Vergara Editor, Buenos Aires, 1992)

28 Ibid The Prince, chapter VII

29 The Catholic Archbishop of Ireland, to whom supposedly two prophecies were revealed during a Peregrination to Rome in 1440. The main prophecy is about the identification ---by mean of slogans--- of the thirty Pontiffs that would govern the Christian Church since the Pope Celestine II (1143-1144).

30 http://en.wikipedia.org/wiki/Prophecy_of_the_Popes

31 Idem

32 Some experts consider that Osama Bin Laden is the Anti Christ and that the reactions of the Islamic countries against the Pope Benedict XVI, and the sexual scandals with children's –by priests of the Catholic Church in United States, London and France- are the first signs of the process…True? False?

33 Wiechowski Siegfried. Historia del Átomo. Publishing Labour, page 69, Barcelona, Spain, 1969

34 To give a simple idea we can highlight that a megaton is equal to a million tons of TNT and a simple missile of the thousands existent today in the world can take a nuclear head of 25 or more megatons, that is to say an enough power to destroy all the cities of a region.

35 The authorities notified officially its decision in this issue in June 2003

36 German General (1780-1831). Was Director of the Berlin School of War; Fought against Napoleon Bonaparte and is recognized as one of the most influential studious of the war as military and political fact. Is author of the concept that recognizes that the war is a simple continuation of the politics by other means.

37 International Monetary Found

38 Military budgets of selected countries 2001, Centre for Defence Information and International Institute for Strategic Studies, U.S. Department of Defence

39 External debt is the debt in foreign currency; internal debt is the debt in the proper currency of each country. United States has a burden debt; but is internal debt because is denominated in it proper currency, the dollar. For that reason United States don't appear as an indebted country in the statistics of the International Monetary Fund.

[40] The World Bank, World Development Indicators 2000, pages 146-149

41 World Bank Development Indicators 2002, and Military Budgets of selected countries 2001; Centre for Defence Information; International Institute for Strategic Studies, London; US Department of Defence

42 International Institute for Strategic Studies, London, The Military Balance 2008, Executive Summary

[43] The Japan revenue per capita was of US $ 35,620 for the year 2000; the China revenue of US $ 840, India 450, Pakistan 440, Iran 1,680 and South Korea 8,910 dollars for the same year. Source: World Bank, World Development Indicators 2002.

Index

Chapter 3

Chapter 4

Second Part
The History

99

Index of tables

57

www.ingramcontent.com/pod-product-compliance
Lightning Source LLC
Chambersburg PA
CBHW070910270326
41927CB00011B/2511